NEW AND COLLECTED POEMS
1950–1980

EX LIBRIS
SUE PEARL

Also by Vernon Scannell

A Mortal Pitch (1957)
Masks of Love (1960)
(*Heinemann Award for Literature 1960*)
A Sense of Danger (1962)
(*Recommended by the Poetry Book Society*)
Walking Wounded (1965)
Epithets of War (1969)
Selected Poems (1971)
The Winter Man (1973)
The Loving Game (1975)
(*Poetry Book Society Choice*)

New & Collected Poems

1950 - 1980

Vernon Scannell

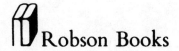 Robson Books

FIRST PUBLISHED IN 1980 BY ROBSON BOOKS
LTD., BOLSOVER HOUSE, 5–6 CLIPSTONE STREET,
LONDON W1P 7EB. COPYRIGHT © VERNON
SCANNELL

First impression 1980
Second impression 1985

British Library Cataloguing in Publication Data

Scannell, Vernon
    New and collected poems, 1950–1980.
    I. Title
    821'.9'14   PR6037.C25

    ISBN 0–86051–104–9
    ISBN 0–86051–105–7 Pbk

Printed and bound in Great Britain by
Biddles Ltd, Guildford and King's Lynn

CONTENTS

Introductory Note   11

A MORTAL PITCH 1957
Something About Art   15
Unsuccessful Poet   15
Two Lessons in Grammar   16
Poets are Never Lovers   18
Posthumous Autobiography   19
They Did Not Expect This   21
Waiting For Night   22
The Lovers Part In Winter   22
London Park in Time of Peace   23
The Visitation   24
How to Fill in A Crossword Puzzle   24
Gunpowder Plot   25
Old Man's Songs   26
Schoolroom on a Wet Afternoon   27
I Grieve for a Lost Land   28
Four Dead Beats to the Bar   29
The Word of Love   29

THE MASK OF LOVE 1960
Romantic Suicide   33
The Lynching   34
Prostitute   34
Remembrance Day   35
Formal Problem   36
Killing Flies   37
Two Appearances   37
Simon Frailman: Ten Sonnets and an Elegiac Coda   38
The Jealous Wife   43

Silver Wedding   44
The Masks of Love   45
Love and Fear   45
First Child   46
Second Child   47
Poem for Jane   48
Jane at Play   48
Sad Story   49

A SENSE OF DANGER 1962
The Terrible Abstractions   53
Act of Violence   53
The Ambush   54
Hearthquake   55
A Sense of Danger   55
Incendiary   56
Death of a Jew   57
Ageing Schoolmaster   57
The Telephone Number   58
Felo de Se   59
The Fair   60
Dead Dog   60
Autobiographical Note   61
The Great War   62
The Men Who Wear my Clothes   63
Juan in Middle Age   64
Incident in a Saloon Bar   64
Wedding   65
Elegy   65
Dejection   66
Howling for Love   67
Cows in Red Pasture   67
A Day on the River   68
The Wicked Words   69
A Sordid Story   70
My Father's Face   71
An Old Lament Renewed   72

WALKING WOUNDED 1965
Autumn   77

Talking of Death   78
Act of Love   78
Telephoning Her   79
It's Sure to End in Tears   80
Voyeur   81
Walking Wounded   81
A Case of Murder   83
Hide and Seek   84
Unacademic Graffiti   85
Report on Drinking Habits   86
Mourning   88
Revenant   88
Since Donovan Died   89
Frankly Speaking: An Interview   89
This Summer   91
Six Year Darling   91
I'm Covered Now   92
A Note for Biographers   93
Moral Problem   94
Millionaire   95
The Great Old Men   96
Love in Any City   97
When We Were Married   98
Taken in Adultery   99
The Old Books   100
Tightrope Walker   100
Peerless Jim Driscoll   101
Time for a Quick One   102
After the Fireworks   103
My Three Hoboes   104
Dirty Story   105
Ruminant   105
My Pen Has Ink Enough   106

EPITHETS OF WAR 1965

Epithets of War   109
Scottsburg USA   113
View from a Wheelchair   114
Uncle Edward's Affliction   115
Any Complaints?   116

A Kind of Hero   117
View from a Deckchair   118
Cigarette   119
View from a Barber's Chair   119
A Song to Celebrate   121
Pistol   121
A Long Sentence   122
The Sunday People   122
Moods of Rain   123
Mercenaries   124
Black Dog   124
Dreamgirl   125
No Sense of Direction   126
Summer in the Park   127
Blood-Letter   127
Growing Pain   128
The Toys of Love   129
A Quaint Disorder   129
A Game of Shove-Ha'penny   130
The Rivals   131
The Moth   132
Wife Killer   132
Death in the Lounge Bar   133
A Simple Need   135
The Mourners   136
Fear of the Dark   137

THE WINTER MAN 1973

Comeback   141
Here and Human   147
The Discriminator   148
The Defrauded Women Speaks   149
Confrontation   150
Love Nest   151
Picture of the Bride   152
Sleeping Beauty   152
A Mystery at Euston   152
The Widow's Complaint   153
Five Domestic Interiors   154
Song for a Winter Birth   155

Cold Spell   156
Picnic on the Lawn   157
End of a Season   158
Beside the Sea   160
Incident at West Bay   161
Battlefields   162
War Cemetery, Ranville   163
The Soldier's Dream   164
Stanley's Dream   165
Charnel House, Rothwell Church   166
Lives of the Poet   167
Legs   168
Six Reasons for Drinking   169
Drunk in Charge   170
Not a Bad Life   171
Polling Day   172
The Winter Man   172

THE LOVING GAME 1975

The Loving Game   179
Wicket Maiden   179
Enemy Agents   180
Where Shall We Go?   180
Separation   181
An Anniversary   182
Marriage Counsel   182
When Love Has Gone   184
Captain Scuttle Ashore   184
Amities   186
Spot-check at Fifty   186
Self-Inflicted Wounds   187
The Wrong of Spring   188
Our Father   189
Wish You Were Here   190
A Circle of Animals and Children   191
Our Pale Daughters   192
Night Music   192
The Cowboy of the Western World   193
Right Dress   193
The Poet's Tongue   194

One That Got Away   194

NEW POEMS 1975–80
    Two Variations on an Old Theme   199
    Old Man in Winter   200
    Reformed Drunkard   201
    A Partial View   202

Introductory Note

For the author the publication of his *Collected Poems* is an unnerving event. He is, in effect, saying: 'This is the best of what I have thought and felt and written from the time when I first began to write verses until the present.' He is uneasily aware that the reviewers may be licking their lips, sharpening their knives and rehearsing their deflatory epigrams. Unlike the author of an isolated slim volume he cannot say: 'Here are a few exercises, an interim report, a record of some tentative steps taken towards the goal of making a complete statement as an artist and as a man. Critics, hold your fire; the best is yet to come!' The author of a Collected Poems is truly on trial for his life.

Well, here I suppose is my life, or the part of it by which I would wish to be judged. In this book I have included all of the pieces that I believe to be, irrespective of their literary quality, genuine poems, that is to say poems which have been written from a sense of compulsion, a real need to explore and articulate experiences which have been important to me. I have jettisoned a great deal, though perhaps not enough. The whole of my first published collection, *Graves and Resurrections* (1948) has been omitted as mere derivative fumbling towards a style. I have cut out those poems which on re-reading seem to be quite obviously false, banal or inept, though I am sure that there will be readers who will find much of what is included just as obviously guilty of these fatal flaws. I have not included any poems which have been written specially for younger readers or commissioned for particular occasions. I fervently, if audaciously, hope that there will be readers who will find something in these pages that will, in Doctor Johnson's words 'enable them the better to enjoy life or the better to endure it'.

A MORTAL PITCH
1957

Something About Art

Easy at first like love:
April of the body and the white-
Gloved constables of conscience all away
On distant busy beats;
Bright shores unplundered and the boats
Nodding at the quay, Come, Come,
It's free! Easy at first
Like life itself, the act
Self-governing, not recognising laws
Beyond fulfilment's need
Or searching for a cause beyond the warm
Compulsion of the April flesh;
Easy like love and life,
Until a dark today
Is suddenly as cold as stone,
And avaricious boatmen on the shore
Extend demanding hands,
While policemen hard as ebony
Hold heavy bruises in gloved paws.
And then like love, like life,
No longer easy as Spring kiss or breath,
His stern vocation points,
And watched on every side
By vigilant and truncheoned laws
He lifts the instrument of art,
In shadow of his conscience and his fate,
Climbs to where the terrible page
White as tomorrow waits.

Unsuccessful Poet

Pity him, even at first when it might seem
That he is not unfortunate; and praise him too.

Puff into the bladder of his self-esteem
And do not underestimate his value:
It is he who demonstrates the hardness of the work
And warns you like a notice where the dangers lurk.

Yes, even when he seems to be happy and strong
Pity him, for like curls and waistlines such happiness is doomed.
The first involuntary yelps that he calls song,
The moments of fragmentary vision and cosmic gloom,
The pinkish rhapsody that celebrates his first erection,
Do not condemn though they don't bear inspection.

For soon you'll see the branch of truth succumb
To the appalling dry-rot of ambition and then
Sad attempts to dress fashionably—on no income.
And after this the first chancre of self-knowledge when
Mind flinches away from the numb and wintry page
Or pen is parched before the barren acreage.

At the age of thirty or thereabouts when he says
That he is a victim of an evil age where all
Standards are debased, remember not to raise
Sceptical brows or blunt instruments; and above all
Do not judge when he goes quietly to his hovel
To put his head in the oven, or write a novel.

Two Lessons in Grammar

I
The Tenses

That which has never happened; holiday
In a glossy land of yellow and blue;
Veiled female beauty; the spicy brew
For which no surpliced barman makes you pay
In cash, disaster, morning recompense;
This you will understand is the Perfect Tense.

The Past Historic? Less easy to describe
Possessing as it does some attributes
Of the Perfect; is a mirror which refutes
Our tentative assumptions with a gibe.
The great boar-hound and girlish pages wander
Through avenues where martyrs, torn asunder,

Leave only dull brown stains and silly skulls,
And headless kings spreadeagled join the stable
Democracy of worm and vegetable.
Obsession with the Past Historic dulls
Those qualities required to understand
The Present which is really where you stand

Unhappily not knowing how to sit
In comfort and compose a farewell letter,
Knowing as well as I, or even better,
Despair's pervasive taste. This incomplete,
Uncertain lesson cannot ease your sense
Of hopelessness. You will smash the Future Tense

II
The Sentence

Perhaps I can make it plain by analogy.
Imagine a machine, not yet assembled,
Each part being quite necessary
To the functioning whole: if the job is fumbled
And a vital piece mislaid
The machine is quite valueless,
The workers will not be paid.

It is just the same when constructing a sentence
But here we must be very careful
And lay stress on the extreme importance
Of defining our terms: nothing is as simple
As it seems at first regard.
'Sentence' might well mean to you
The amorous rope or twelve years' hard.

No, by 'sentence' we mean, quite simply, words
Put together like the parts of a machine.
Now remember we must have a verb: verbs
Are words of action like Murder, Love, or Sin.
But these might be nouns, depending
On how you use them—
Already the plot is thickening.

Except when the mood is imperative; that is to say
A command is given like Pray, Repent, or Forgive
(Dear me, these lessons get gloomier every day)
Except, as I was saying, when the mood is gloomy—
                    I mean imperative,
We need nouns, or else of course
Pronouns: words like Maid,
Man, Wedding or Divorce.

A sentence must make sense. Sometimes I believe
Our lives are ungrammatical. I guess that some of you
Have misplaced the direct object: the longer I live
The less certain I feel of anything I do.
But now I begin
To digress. Write down these simple sentences:—
I am sentenced: I love: I murder: I sin.

Poets are Never Lovers

Poets are never really lovers;
If they were they would not need
To press between ambitious covers
Records of the lover's deed,
Or agonise to make the fervent
Sigh or grunt more eloquent.

Not being lovers they can see
More clearly than the fortunate
Speechless who record the glee

And glory under passionate
Eiderdowns, as gay as birds,
That love is lovelier than words.

Just as the pauper knows the power
Of the fat man's casual wad,
Or fainting in his dizzy tower
Of hunger makes of food his god,
The loveless poet alone in bed
Gauges the fortune of the fed.

Manhandling language is his job,
A task not suitable for lovers
Whose passion fattens on each sob;
And yet he does not envy others,
Unless the words turn dead as stone,
Leaving him dungeoned, and alone.

Posthumous Autobiography

Once I was a hero,
Slashing the grimy enemies who groaned
And churned their frantic fear before my calm
Fury, watched them beg for sweet reprieve
On broken knees, bawling round and loud
Beneath my blade of little ones at home.
And some I spared, mingling in my smile
Admixture of compassion and contempt.
With bandage bloody-badged upon my brow
Returned to let the English sun bring out
Brilliant blooms of medals on my breast
For favoured dainty virgins to admire.
Yes, once I was a hero but
The bombs began to fall.

Once I was a sailor
Swinging with the loll and roll at night,
Hearing the slap and wallop of the water
On creaking timbered sides; and when I slept
The fishes glided round my glassy skull.
Then when the storm enraged the grunting sea
Into a foaming epileptic fit
The ship a monstrous bronco bucked and lurched
To each enormous heave and I alone,
The only one not spewing helplessly,
Replaced the skipper on the howling bridge,
Staring the tumult out rode safely home.
Yes, once I was a sailor but
The ship put out to sea.

Once I was a lover
Walking avenues of blushes and of sighs,
Singing at night hot arias that flushed
The upper casements with a yearning light.
My bootleg kisses sent a red-head wild
Who drowned herself when I refused to smile.
Five brunettes took vows, and thirteen blondes
Wept away their beauty when I rode
Away one casual evening with a wave
Of that instructive and omniscient hand
That each had worshipped and enshrined in dream.
Yes, once I was a lover but
A woman came to bed.

Once I was a poet
Breaking the silence with an axe of bright
Articulate anger, crunching cant and lies
Between sharp lyric teeth and shrugging all
The green and silent nightingales away.
And once I was a pale religious man
My soul and conscience laundered perfectly
As white as birthday cake: rebellious psalms
Began to sing my name and when I breathed
The air about my haloed head was faint

With sweetest incense; steeples belled my name.
Yes, once I was a poet and religious,
But the terrible angels called on me.
Once I was alive.

They Did Not Expect This

They did not expect this. Being neither wise nor brave
And wearing only the beauty of youth's season
They took the first turning quite unquestioningly
And walked quickly without looking back even once.

It was of course the wrong turning. First they were nagged
By a small wind that tugged at their clothing like a dog;
Then the rain began and there was no shelter anywhere,
Only the street and the rows of houses stern as soldiers.

Though the blood chilled, the endearing word burnt the tongue.
There were no parks or gardens or public houses:
Midnight settled and the rain paused leaving the city
Enormous and still like a great sleeping seal.

At last they found accommodation in a cold
Furnished room where they quickly learnt to believe in ghosts;
They had their hope stuffed and put on the mantelpiece
But found, after a while, that they did not notice it.

While she spends many hours looking in the bottoms of teacups
He reads much about association football
And waits for the marvellous envelope to fall:
Their eyes are strangers and they rarely speak.
                              They did not expect this.

Waiting for Night

Here, in the clattering day where the street rings
With showers of glittering coins from the rich sun,
One walks, dazed with the bootleg warmth, emboldened
By the gay behaviour of the young. High-hung
Above the rakish roofs and kitchen gardens
The white sheets puff their chests towards the sun,
Proud as clouds of the marriage beds they honour.
And in the park's remarkable new green,
Bright and dainty as confectioner's wares
Girls wander where the lazy deckchairs lean
Striped like the humbugs of a child's desire.
Children are there, the reckless fire-eaters
Licking the solid flame from yellow torches,
Throwing the light grenades of vocal sound
For the pure joy of hearing the explosion.

But there is one who is no longer young,
For whom this annual resurrection brings
Only the sense of loss. Waiting for night
To draw soft blinds across the mirrors of
Shopwindows and the girls' indifferent eyes;
Waiting for night, his own and treacherous eyes
Kneel down before the royal sun and rest,
Pretending to a true allegiance;
Waiting for night when hate can walk upright,
And he can crush the lovers that his feet encounter
And bite their silver moon to prove it counterfeit.

The Lovers Part In Winter

It seemed appropriate that it should happen
On the day when winter consolidated
Its territorial gains; when the sky's skin
Was tight with the pain of cold and all the streams
Were paralysed, still, like a photograph.

Separately they'll hate the winter from now on,
Find its beauty not their style at all,
Hating the air in which the germ of lie
Could not for an instant live. They will fear
That mass of frozen thunder, the mountain range.

The green conspirators were dead or banished,
There was no talk of bird or resurrection;
Speech lay betrayed in fragments at their feet;
The bed was cold as snow, the fire was out
And stillborn tears froze hard and cut like glass.

They had both been cruel and dishonest;
Yet pity hurt like winter when she went
Over the snow alone. And then it seemed
Her scarlet cloak, laced by the falling flakes,
Grew ermine-white except for stains of blood.

London Park in Time of Peace

On the blue breast of August bravely burns
The medallion of the polished sun,
White tourniquets of cloud conceal the wounds
Incurred in wintry battles of attrition.

The children's laughter rises like the bright
And liberated kites; adventures rock
At landing-stages waiting for the right
Adventurer to enter; lovers shock

The tight-lipped woman who, accompanied
By all she knows of love on leather leash,
Walks in the glass enclosure of despair
Towards the fragile certainty of tea.

And the iron soldier on the pompous horse
Stares upward, showing neither fear nor wonder;
The stormcloud, turgid, purple, ripe as plum,
Waits for the raping teeth of burly thunder.

The Visitation

The fire is small and hushed, the candles' speech
Is muted to a whisper while the walls
Tremble, move closer, then nervously withdraw;
Somewhere, beyond this world, a nightbird calls.

The clock counts moments in its neat black voice,
The wind complains that night is cruel to him;
Small pools of darkness brim the shallow vales
Delved in the white plain of the counterpane.

The bed seems strangely large, the intricate
Carved posts are parodied by aggravated
Semblances that mime upon the ceiling;
Only the pillowed head is unrelated.

Only the old frail skull and waxen hands
That rest upon the counterpane seem certain,
Indifferent to the terror that informs
The room's hysteria, the frightened curtain.

The noiseless gibberish of shadows grows
More feverish; bird calls from night's dark hill
Imperious; the candles weep, the fire burns low,
The clock is ticking but the hands are still.

How to Fill in a Crossword Puzzle

First adjust your spectacles and take your pen,
(A pencil will serve equally well) and pick the easiest clue:
Here you are: five letters down—'What is Man?'
Clown, Rogue, Beast, or even Saint would do.

Now let's try another going across. Here is one
Which seems more likely than the rest: 'Lethal but Sweet,'

A six-letter word, the first of which is B
If Beast were right for man—the beast with two feet.

Think hard—Lethal but Sweet. Assuming Beast is correct,
Breast might fit, the sweet but bladed breast
Of her you hugged, who bled you white and stabbed
To death your groping heart most treacherously.

If, as may well be, you have mistakenly put Beast
Adjustments are required unless you are going to let
This chequered puzzle stay unsolved. Try Rogue instead of Beast,
Then 'Lethal but Sweet,' could reasonably be Regret.

Of course the word Clown would fit the first clue you attempted
(Yes, I admit this puzzle is confusing)
Then your six-letter word going across might be
Coitus, Create, Cringe or possibly Crying.

The other word, less likely I suppose, is Saint.
Here the thing 'Lethal but Sweet' would begin with S.
Sinful it might be, Senses or simply Seduce.
The snag about these clues is the alternatives are endless.

Write in the words faintly because you may have to alter them,
And be warned. When the puzzle is solved, and like a satisfied
                                                        lover
You lean back sighing and sleepy, then you will find
That the black squares hide the secrets you will never uncover.

Gunpowder Plot

For days these curious cardboard buds have lain
In brightly coloured boxes. Soon the night
Will come. We pray there'll be no sullen rain
To make these magic orchids flame less bright.

Now in the garden's darkness they begin
To flower; the frenzied whizz of Catherine-wheel
Puts forth its fiery petals and the thin
Rocket soars to burst upon the steel

Bulwark of a cloud. And then the guy,
Absurdly human phoenix, is again
Gulped by greedy flames: the harvest sky
Is flecked with threshed and glittering golden grain.

'Uncle! A cannon! Watch me as I light it!'
The women, helter-skelter, squealing high,
Retreat; the paper fuse is quickly lit,
A cat-like hiss and spit of fire, a sly

Falter, then the air is shocked with blast.
The cannon bangs, and in my nostrils drifts
A bitter scent that brings the lurking past
Lurching to my side. The present shifts,

Allows a ten-year memory to walk
Unhindered now; and so I'm forced to hear
The banshee howl of mortar and the talk
Of men who died; am forced to taste my fear.

I listen for a moment to the guns,
The torn earth's grunts, recalling how I prayed.
The past retreats. I hear a corpse's sons:
'Who's scared of bangers?' 'Uncle! John's afraid!'

Old Man's Song

The baby bawling, being sick,
The spotty girl with hockey-stick
Who dreams of pink blancmange and pie,
Might not be
Ideally

Happy but I know they are
Far better off than I.

I watch the warm limbs jolly by,
Feel neither grand nor fatherly:
I don't long
For those strong
Bodies but how achingly
I desire desire.

Friday night boys as bold as Bass
Release their lusts like poison gas
In punching yells or foggy songs;
That in the end
They will descend
To my cellar does not ease
This thorny hat of wrongs.

The autumn leaves romantically
Die gay and suicidally
And night is hurt by the owl's cry;
The still sleeper
Sleeps deeper
Whom no alarming clock will shock:
He's better off than I.

Cat in the night clawing silence
Howling lust that needs no licence
Makes me want to want to die;
Even though
They don't know
Dogs and bitches bogged in ditches
Are far better off than I.

Schoolroom on a Wet Afternoon

The unrelated paragraphs of morning
Are forgotten now: the severed heads of kings

Rot by the misty Thames; the roses of York
And Lancaster are pressed between the leaves
Of history; negroes sleep in Africa.
The complexities of simple interest lurk
In inkwells and the brittle sticks of chalk:
Afternoon is come and English Grammar.

Rain falls as though the sky has been bereaved,
Stutters its inarticulate grief on glass
Of every lachrymose pane. The children read
Their books or make pretence of concentration,
Each bowed head seems bent in supplication
Or resignation to the fate that waits
In the unmapped forests of the future.
Is it their doomed innocence noon weeps for?

In each diminutive breast a human heart
Pumps out the necessary blood: desires,
Pains and ecstasies surfride each singing wave
Which breaks in darkness on the mental shores.
Each child is disciplined; absorbed and still
At his small desk. Yet lift the lid and see,
Amidst frayed books and pencils, other shapes:
Vicious rope, glaring blade, the gun cocked to kill.

I Grieve for a Lost Land

I grieve for a lost land as the gulls swim
Easily on air, parodying pain
With their outrageous cries:
I grieve for a lost land as the dark stain
Of night spreads over the sad skies
And the gulls drift into silence on a chill wind.

And later, when the sea's great engines roar
Ceaselessly of death and exile, I recall
Nights starred with promises

Of a bright morning's golden madrigal
And skies blue as the nursery boys
Who blew their silver trumpets when the cows were in corn.

I grieve for a lost land which lies beyond
This sea which tells its hunger to the night
And shakes its rags of foam
For the idiot moon's remote delight;
I grieve for a dead child, a lost wand,
A shore to which no exile may return.

Four Dead Beats to the Bar

While day still was, four dead beats to the bar repaired,
Wearing their sultry thirsts at a Saturday angle,
Each clothed in melancholy's threadbare mantle
And the bright unenviable medals of despair.

Later they sang: blew bawdy songs from blubbery lips
Like gaudy bubbles, braved the ticking cannonade;
Toasted their toasts, composed a purple serenade
To every maid and bar, to all the whores and hips.

Then thin bells squealed that there must be no light,
No drink, nor any serenading from henceforth;
And four dead beats to a drunken rhythm waltzed
Out to be swallowed by the panting thirsty night.

The Word of Love

Perhaps it found its perfect expression
Early in life, in the fairy-tale time,
Concerning itself with a character out of fiction,
The sleeping princess or glittering snow queen,

Or focused mutely and profoundly on
A furry bear whose solitary eye was a sad button.

Certainly, as I grew tall and gruff
And the blood of the bear turned into straw
I somehow lost the habit of love.
The leggy girls, whose sharp heels tore
My flimsy dreams, with laughter crushed
The flower at the heart of my lunar lust.

Uncertain now, myopic with peering
At celluloid legends and paper lies,
The one word breaks on my disbelieving;
And yet, and yet, the dumb heart bears
The syllable like a child in its stillness
And your present absence is a mortal illness.

THE MASKS OF LOVE
1960

Romantic Suicide

He was not wicked, merely wrong,
Always wrong whatever he did,
And when he fell in love the song
He sang was pitched too high and loud
Offending those white ears he loved.
And when she went he bravely hid
His grief and walked into the water,
For that was what the poems he read
Said was the appropriate thing
To do if you had lost your lover.
He did not know the world of rhyme
Has laws outside the world of time
And what is beautiful in verse
May well outside be anything
But beautiful, indeed far worse
Than images whose conscious aim
It is to sicken and alarm.
And so he sank into the lake
And wallowed with the perch and pike
Among green wavering scenery.
Seven days were lost before they hauled
His corpse from lecherous weeds and mud,
And we who gathered there to see
That romantic suicide
Saw a fat inflated blubber,
A thing composed of greyish rubber.
His face we will not dwell upon
Though creatures in the waters had
No such pretty scruples there.
Enough to say we turned away,
And what pity might have touched
Our hearts was swamped by nausea.
All we could do was dumbly pray
That God prove less fastidious:
Extend his mercy, sweet and strong,
To one not wicked, merely wrong.

The Lynching

They rode back in trap or Ford or Cadillac.
Behind them on the tree upon the hill
Beneath the non-committal dark
Star-punctured sky their deed hung still
And black. They rode fast. One might have thought
That they were being pursued; their speed
Lunged forward with a long arm through the night
To drag the small town to their need.
And in the town the white wives in their white
Nightgowns listened to the clock
And with their wide-eyed fingers plucked
Those gowns which, fastened at the neck
And neat at feet, need not be roughed that night
To prove their husbands' manhood, or the lack.

Prostitute

All your endearments and the charms you offer,
Bulge of breast and buttock, trumpet eye,
Shall not persuade the night you do not suffer
The blade that hurts but does not purify
All your endearments and the charms you offer.

After the dark manoeuvres you may play
A few pale hours with beady words like Beauty,
While locks and curtains thwart the indigent day
And coppers are engaged on other duty:
After the dark manoeuvres you may play.

Always for you the bed meant painful labour,
But not a natal labour crowned with love;
The sheets evoke with stain and faintest odour
Nostalgia you put on like a glove;
Always for you the bed meant painful labour.

The bed, your business, factory of lust,
For other people wears a different guise
Unless the cinema abused your trust;
.The dreaming virgin would not recognise
The bed, your business, factory of lust.

The vicar's pious pity is maltreated;
Your laughter like bright scissors rips it up;
Primeval sin is not to be defeated
By magic wafer or the sacred cup;
The vicar's pious pity is maltreated.

And all the endearments and the charms you offer,
The wicked stars remark them being drunk
Nightly by Time who, like a pimping lover,
Robs your white factory except for junk—
The obsolete endearments you will offer.

Remembrance Day

Apposite blood red the blobs
Of artificial poppies count
Our annual dead.
The garment of lament is worn
Threadbare and each medal hangs
Heavy its shameful head.

Bugles make their sad assault
Upon the heart and spine and throat
Ordering regret.
The names evoked are usual:
Passchendaele, Bapaume and Loos—
Our cheeks are wet.

And fumbling for the right response
We summon names more personal:
Nobby, Frank and Ted.

But wormy years have eaten their
Identities and none can mourn
These artificial dead.

And when a true emotion strikes
It strikes a crude, unsanctioned blow
Which brings a harsher chill
To hearts that know that they grow old
And must grow older yet before
That terrible Until.

Formal Problem

The poet, in his garden, holds his pen
Like a dart between two fingers and a thumb;
The target is unfortunately blurred;
He does not see as clearly as when young,
Or, rather, doubt and nervousness obtrude:
He dare not risk the unreflecting fling.

How to convey the taste and texture of
This sun-drunk afternoon? How can he sieve
The essence of these greens, the grass, the trees,
The mating scents, the way the clouds behave,
And shape it to a pattern which might please
The glinting intellect and hungry Five?

And how include the aeroplane which slides
No larger than a pearl across the skies,
Its roar wrapped up in distance which conceals
A figure masked and helmeted whose strong
Finger stabs the button that resolves
The poet's problem in a flash, and bang.

Killing Flies

Compelled by their black hum
And accidental mischief, I,
Distracted from my pompous play
With words that twist and tease,
Rolled myself a paper club
And stalked my quick tormentors round
The room until they settled on
The wall, their mortuary slab.
Three I translated with one swipe
From busy bodies into dark
Smudges on my wall
Before I knew my action wrong
And guiltily let fall
The paper truncheon and went back
To where my words like insects bled
And dried upon their paper shroud,
All dead, unquestionably dead.

Two Appearances

The lean ecstatic man, the starry poet,
Expecting any day the total vision
And generously preparing to bestow it
On all of us, despite some mild derision
From that minority who doubtless find
His meditative beauty not their kind,
Walks whitely like a batsman to his crease;
While in the dirty night the ugly fellow,
His barrel belly resting on his thighs,
Calls out the temptress with a soundless bellow
And fixes her with angry bloodshot eyes,
Then forces her to bear a masterpiece.

Simon Frailman:

Ten Sonnets and an Elegiac Coda

First Sight

Simon Frailman, six feet in his dreams,
A thickening five feet eight when morning rings
And pricks him with insistent questionings:
Why did he never wear those uniforms,
The plumage and caparisons, bear arms
Or, over one heroic nipple, wings?
And now it is too late. The evening brings
A smoky sadness to the mortgaged lawns.

A moderate man with no intemperate lusts,
Content to tame the rose and civilise
The lawless strawberry, he guards the trust
Of wife and children and will never slip
The marriage leash; his quaint adulteries
Performed with lawful spouse at his thick hip.

Simon on Sunday

Printed rumours rustle through the morning.
The fragrant chamber music of the bacon
Is drowned by richer chords of roast and pudding
As Simon sprays and weeds his timid garden.
The spectres of the earlier bells compel
A melancholy that is hard to pardon
While birds in shimmering trees are simmering still
And thin stems bend beneath their fragile burden.

Evening is listless, fat with Monday morning;
Time tells its dirty secret to the heart;
The fiddles and the saxophones are moaning
As venal meat is prinked with spurious art.
A sudden chill knifes Simon to the bone:
He sees a waiting Sunday, barren as a stone.

Simon Drunk . . .

'It's not too late,' the glass says to his lips;
'It's not too late,' the whisper in the bowel.
The glasses wink and chink, the cigarettes
Are wagging words, but Simon draws apart.
He will be Gauguin, paint outrageous tarts,
Learn Greek, read Proust and do P.T. each day;
Write a witty novel or a play
And lead the leading lady well astray.

'It's not too late,' his lips say to his glass.
He feels the fireworks flowering in the dark
Beneath his sober shirt. He'll tell his boss
Just what he thinks of him and find some work
In Paris, Athens, Rome. . . . Then Mrs. Frailman spoke:
'The Party's over, Simon. Let's go home.'

. . . And Simon Sober

An ashen dawn begins in Simon's mouth.
The conscious day unglues his sleep to drop
Some broken recollections in his lap
And snigger with unsympathetic mirth.
He sees himself, absurd, immodest, vain,
Swaying from maudlin right to left of wrath,
Exciting pursed contempt or nervous ruth,
His dignity, like trousers, fallen down.

The day, a soft groan, greys towards its end
Sustained by aspirin and Worcester Sauce;
A misty sexuality, a wind
Of speechless longing drifts towards his sleep
Where he, marooned upon a small remorse,
Builds resolutions he will never keep.

The Good Temptation

Frailman alone, peaceful in the sweet
Tobacco educating simple air,
Feels a spectral elbow nudge the heart

And knows what Newman knew when tempted by
Not venery but virtue, holy snare
Which draws the chosen victim to the high
Pinnacle which looks upon the wheat
Immortal and the golden everywhere.

Yet how resistible temptation of this sort.
Soon spirit aches and squints at such a glare,
And Simon turns away upon the thought
Of leaving his terrain to sojourn there
Where he may never see, or need to see,
The white and delicate legs move winkingly.

Simon Perplexed

Then Simon thinks how difficult to feel
Real love when there is no reflected pleasure,
And knows he never could sincerely kneel
To intercede for one who had his measure.

He might whip up a plausible compassion
For those whose sins are operatic, loud,
Or those whose moral dress is out of fashion,
Whose bloody heads are tinted but unbowed.

But not a simulacrum of affection
Can he display for virtue's household guard
Whose faces, even after resurrection,
Would still resemble watchful bags of lard.

And Simon swears if these are such as dwell
In Paradise, then heaven must be pure hell.

Father

Owl tinctured, blind, the wind sighs through the night,
Then mimics, with a sudden lift, a cry
Of infant fear, and Simon sits upright,
Pricked quick by this pathetic fallacy.
But none, alas, of Frailman's children now
Perturbs the evening with needs sad or shrill:

Two crude and violent boys, both low of brow,
A ten-year girl of double-barrelled will.

They do not need him now to heave them out
Of wells of furry fear or scare away
With one electric slap the grunting snout
That sniffed their beds: yet if they should display
A leaf of love his pleasure is immense
And humble from the heart's intelligence.

Simon sans Teeth

This is a stage from which there's no retreat,
Thinks Simon sadly; the lost familiars leave
A sibilance that hisses of senility;
His smile is false indeed. He cannot eat.
And Mrs. Frailman and his friends deceive
Themselves, not him, when they repeatedly
Assure him that, before much longer, he
Will treat them as his own, contemptuously.

But though, for work, these teeth prove adequate
He knows and always will that they are false.
A part of him has died and, soon or late,
The rest of him must follow till that hour
When he can buy no artificial pulse
And his dead grin will gleam in some dark drawer.

Birthday Present

Forty-six years since Simon bawled his first
And unavailing no at being forced
To put on short mortality and thrust
His midget head through life's enormous noose
Which now, perceptibly, is much less loose.

He once believed his rampant greed and lust
Would leave their ageing cage or that, at least,
They'd drowse replete, resavouring the past;
And he would hang his fears and vanity
Upon a hook in dim serenity.

But through the jungle of his nerves the lithe
And tigerish beauties creep; now he could swear,
Until the rope of years pulls tight, he'll writhe
And hear the wanton whisperings everywhere.

Simon Gay

No causing in the sky or envelope
But joy, like oxygen, is everywhere;
And though he knows a hostile periscope
May surface soon and fix him with its glare
He rides the sparkling crest and flies his smile,
Gay in the face of preying buccaneers;
And though the clouds may shortly belch with bile
He will not shut his eyes or plug his ears.

These spells are brief and magical. He knows
Before the day is out he'll run aground
Or be capsized by envious torpedoes
Then cast up on some chill barbaric isle:
Yet Simon vows, though grievous reefs abound,
Whatever comes, the voyage is well worth while.

Elegiac Coda

And when the wingèd chariot at last
Accelerates and runs him down, what then?
No melancholy flags will sag half-mast,
The pubs will close at the usual half-past ten;
The lions in the square will be dry eyed;
No newspaper will note that he has died.

But Frailman's children, burly now or tall,
Will find with slight astonishment that he
Bequeaths, with lesser valuables, a small
And wholly disconcerting legacy:
A foliate grief that opens like a fist
To show a love they doubted could exist.

And Mrs. Frailman, staring at a chair,
Whose occupant contrives by not being there

To occupy it far more poignantly
Than when his flesh flopped in it wearily,
Will know that he has cleared a way which she
Must follow after, that more easily.

The Jealous Wife

Like a private eye she searches
For clues through diaries and papers;
Examines his clothing for the guilty stains
Of crimson lipstick, wicked wine,
Or something biological.
And when no act of sensual
Crime can be at length surmised
She is most puzzled and surprised
To be assailed by disappointment
Not relief. Her steel intent
Is never to betray to him
The blonde and naked thoughts within
The purple bedroom of her mind,
But her resolve can never stand
The pressure of the need to know:
'Where?' she says and 'When?' and 'Who?'
'What time?' 'What day?' The question-marks
Like powerful iron grappling hooks
Drag him to her fantasy.
And then he cannot fail to see
Within the harem of her skull
The lovely wickednesses loll.
Thus, at night, they softly creep,
Tap at the darkened panes of sleep;
Then, white and tender, glide inside
His dream on whose delightful slope
At last her fears are justified.

Silver Wedding

The party is over and I sit among
The flotsam that its passing leaves,
The dirty glasses and fag-ends:
Outside, a black wind grieves.

Two decades and a half of marriage;
It does not really seem as long,
And yet I find I have scant knowledge
Of youth's ebullient song.

David, my son, my loved rival,
And Julia, my tapering daughter,
Now grant me one achievement only:
I turn their wine to water.

And Helen, partner of all these years,
Helen my spouse, my sack of sighs,
Reproaches me for every hurt
With injured bovine eyes.

There must have been passion once, I grant,
But neither she nor I could bear
To have its ghost come prowling from
Its dark and frowsy lair.

And we, to keep our nuptials warm,
Still wage sporadic, fireside war;
Numb with insult each yet strives
To scratch the other raw.

Twenty-five years we've now survived;
I'm not sure either why or how
As I sit with a wreath of quarrels set
On my tired and balding brow.

The Masks of Love

We did not understand that it was there,
The love we hungered for; it even seemed
Love's enemies, indifference, distaste
And cruelty, informed our father's stare
Of pained reproof, the homiletic tongue,
The sudden rage, and mother's graven face;
But we were wrong.
And when the chalk-faced master showed his teeth
And pickled us in hurtful verbiage
We labelled him Misanthropos and swore
That his vocation was revenge. But this
Was not the truth.
And later, when the easy woman gave
Free scholarship to study at the warm
College of her flesh, we called her coarse,
Promiscuous, and cunning to behave
With subsequent incontinent remorse.
We thought that we were lucky to evade
Her plot to eat us up alive, but we
Were just about as wrong as we could be.
As afterwards we were, when our sweet dove
That we had welcomed to the marriage cote
Became a beaky squawker and appeared
To loathe the bargain that her instincts bought:
And we did not permit her to reveal
The tender fingers in the iron glove
Like that whose knuckled stratagems conceal
A desperate and brooding love.

Love and Fear

This love has conjured up catastrophes:
And where my loved one walks each whispering hedge

Conceals an ambush and a levelled threat.
All dangers sidle to her trusting side;
I know contagion will be sure to covet
The breathing pastures of her tender flesh.

Disaster trumpets up reserves all over,
Calls traffic accidents beneath his flag;
Assassins pace the pavement where she idles;
Death pants with lust and trembles like a dog.
I cannot bear to have her leave my sight
To face the menace of my luck and love.

And will this fear, this bully of the heart
Grow with my love? This seems most probable,
And lovers fail because they cannot live
With that enormous beast, and cease to love.
Therefore I fear to lose this precious fear,
And cherish it, as her I hold so dear.

First Child

FOR JOHN AND JEAN BOURNE

What fed their apprehension was the fears
Of loud compulsory insomnia,
Their little liberties abruptly cancelled,
The marvel of their marriage darkening
Beneath a wagging, sanitary bunting:
All these intrusions they would have to face.
But when the niggling interdicts and chill
Labours took up threatened residence
These seemed to be quite friendly after all.

What they had not prepared themselves to meet
Was this: the soft catastrophes, the sly
Menaces whose names are hard to spell
Creeping to her cot, the quiet killers
Loading their white guns and brooding over
That innocent and O, so fragile head.

Second Child

The world, contracted to your needs,
Receives you now, is hushed and warm
But wider than the womb.
As in a stream the sketchy weeds
Waver, your voice in silence floats
And summons instantly white flights
Of tendernesses to your room.

Soon your world will widen, noise
Grow big and blunder through the cool
Cavern where you coo-ing curl
And crow your elementary joys.
Then pain and fear will bully you
Nor may your parents rescue you
At once from that bleak school.

For them you bring gay spurts of flowers,
But also bitter herbs and grave
Auguries that they must grieve
As well as praise your ripening powers
Which open weeping gates and doors
Leading to the perilous days
And quays whence ships of exile leave.

And yet, dear egomaniac,
They would not wish you anywhere
But in the harbour of their care.
Your being there has healed a lack
And even more: love's little space
Has been extended and the harsh
Destructive seas forced back a pace.

Poem for Jane

So many catalogues have been
Compiled by poets, good and bad,
Of qualities that they would wish
To see their infant daughters wear;
Or lacking children they have clad
Others' daughters in the bright
Imagined garments of the flesh,
Prayed for jet or golden hair
Or for the inconspicuous
Homespun of the character
That no one ever whistles after.
Dear Jane, whatever I may say
I'm sure approving whistles will
Send you like an admiral on
Ships of welcome in a bay
Of tender waters where the fish
Will surface longing to be meshed
Among the treasure of your hair.
And as for other qualities
There's only one I really wish
To see you amply manifest
And that's a deep capacity
For loving; and I long for this
Not for any lucky one
Who chances under your love's sun
But because, without it, you
Would never know completely joy
As I know joy through loving you.

Jane at Play

I watch her in the garden and enjoy
Her serious enjoyment as she bends

And murmurs her grave nonsense to the toy
Circle of her animals and friends;
The doll that she quite obviously likes best
Would be to other eyes the ugliest.

For it is only later that we choose
To favour things which publish our good taste,
Whose beauty proves our talent to refuse
To dote upon the comic or defaced;
Unlike the child who needs no reference
Or cautious map to find her preference.

Yet we may be deceived by some old trick,
Robbed of our bright expensive instruments
And bundled from our path into the thick
Frondescence strangling all our arguments,
As when we see our child's plain loveliness
And blunder blind into our happiness.

Sad Story

Once upon a tomb this story closes,
A green page scrawled with a signature of roses.

She could not live with life between
Her and her love who lay unseen

And partnered only by the white
And bony gentry in the night.

Once upon a time the tale began
Of a woman who loved a death-loved man.

And so it ends upon a tomb;
A frozen bride and silent groom.

A SENSE OF DANGER
1962

The Terrible Abstractions

The naked hunter's fist, bunched round his spear,
Was tight and wet inside with sweat of fear;
He heard behind him what the hunted hear.

The silence in the undergrowth crept near;
Its mischief tickled in his nervous ear
And he became the prey, the quivering deer.

The naked hunter feared the threat he knew:
Being hunted, caught, then slaughtered like a ewe
By beasts who padded on four legs or two.

The naked hunter in the bus or queue
Under his decent wool is frightened too
But not of what his hairy forebear knew.

The terrible abstractions prowl about
The compound of his fear and chronic doubt;
He keeps fires burning boldly all night through,
But cannot keep the murderous shadows out.

Act of Violence

Flight (pursuit by only fear)
Beats on the pavement and invades the ear.
The sagging victim like a children's guy
Is dumped in the gutter. One pale cry
Flutters a moment and is blotted out.
A life has leaked away with that frail shout.
The simmering night refuses to ask why
Or who it was that had to die.
The stiff policemen will in time appear;
'In time,' I said, but let me make it clear:

In time to scent and stalk their prey,
Not save the victim for a flowering day.
This time tomorrow either mop or rain
Will certainly have wiped away the stain
That crudely signs the cold page of the street,
And I shall hide my head beneath the sheet
And mutter midnight spells to keep away
The vision of the streetlamp's bilious ray
Lighting both faces undisguised,
And recognized, and recognized.

The Ambush

Noise paled, gradual or quick, I cannot say,
And I became aware of silence everywhere;
I sucked it in when I breathed in the air.

Silence lay inside my lungs and heart
And in my brain. And with the silence came
A stillness such as paintings would disclaim.

This rural scene was not a work of art:
The fallen tree lay in real bluebells while
It played at being an actual crocodile.

The sky was real, the brambles like barbed wire
Would scratch and snag the clothing or the skin;
This Surrey wood seemed one for wandering in.

But I did not go in, though I had meant to.
I waited for a whisper, cry or screech.
The whole green parliament had stifled speech.

Irresolute I waited there until
The hostile death of noise sent me away;
I swore that I'd return on a more propitious day.

But safe in the dangerous noises of the city
I knew I'd never know what thing hid there,
What voiceless incarnation of despair

Or vigilant guerilla lying still,
With breath indrawn among the ferns and dirt,
Waiting to attack or be dealt his mortal hurt.

Hearthquake

A week has passed without a word being said:
No headlines, though that's natural, I suppose
Since there were no injured, let alone dead,
Yet I expected a paragraph or so.
But no, not even comment passed in bars,
No gossip over fences while shirts flap
And sheets boast on the line like sails on spars,
And yet it happened: I can swear to that.
I remember it as if it were last night,
My sitting smug and cosy as a cat
Until the carpet suddenly took fright
And bucked beneath my feet. Walls winced. The clock
Upon the mantelpiece began to dance;
The photograph of me aged twenty-one fell flat;
Glass cracked. The air went cold with shock.
I did not sleep at all well through that night
Nor have I since. I cannot understand
Why no one—not my nearest neighbour even—
Refers to what occurred on that strange evening
Unless, in some way difficult to see,
He is afraid to mention it. Like me.

A Sense of Danger

The city welcomed us. Its favoured sons,
Holders of office, prosperous and plump

With meat and honours, said, 'Put down your guns,
There's nothing here to fear. The industrial slump,
The Plague, the hunting-packs, the underfed,
All are gone, all caged or safely dead.

'Rest easy here. Put down your loads and stay,
And we will purify you with the kiss
Of sweet hygienic needles and display
Incredible varieties of bliss;
We'll strip your inhibitions off like trousers.
Relax. Don't brood. You'll be as safe as houses.'

But we declined, took up our guns and bags;
Turning blind backs on offers of delight
Left for the gaunt terrain and squinting crags;
With luck we'd find a water hole that night.
'As safe as houses,' they had called the town;
But we had seen great houses tumbled down.

Incendiary

That one small boy with a face like pallid cheese
And burnt-out little eyes could make a blaze
As brazen, fierce and huge, as red and gold
And zany yellow as the one that spoiled
Three thousand guineas' worth of property
And crops at Godwin's Farm on Saturday
Is frightening—as fact and metaphor:
An ordinary match intended for
The lighting of a pipe or kitchen fire
Misused may set a whole menagerie
Of flame-fanged tigers roaring hungrily.
And frightening, too, that one small boy should set
The sky on fire and choke the stars to heat
Such skinny limbs and such a little heart
Which would have been content with one warm kiss
Had there been anyone to offer this.

Death of a Jew

He wore a monocle of blood.
The crimson ribbon ran
Down one wax cheek.
His teeth had been kicked in.

Close by, on the pavement, lay
His crunched pince-nez;
The lard-fat moon ignored
His scatterbrain black grin.

The drumbeat tramping faded
Like a dying pulse;
He did not seem to hear it,
Or anything else:

But lay on the pavement grinning,
His toothless jaws wide;
And another crimson ribbon
Crawled from his side.

Ageing Schoolmaster

And now another autumn morning finds me
   With chalk dust on my sleeve and in my breath,
Preoccupied with vague, habitual speculation
   On the huge inevitability of death.

Not wholly wretched, yet knowing absolutely
   That I shall never reacquaint myself with joy,
I sniff the smell of ink and chalk and my mortality
   And think of when I rolled, a gormless boy,

And rollicked round the playground of my hours,
   And wonder when precisely tolled the bell

Which summoned me from summer liberties
    And brought me to this chill autumnal cell

From which I gaze upon the april faces
    That gleam before me, like apples ranged on shelves,
And yet I feel no pinch or prick of envy
    Nor would I have them know their sentenced selves.

With careful effort I can separate the faces,
    The dull, the clever, the various shapes and sizes,
But in the autumn shades I find I only
    Brood upon death, who carries off all the prizes.

The Telephone Number

Searching for a lost address I find,
Among dead papers in a dusty drawer,
A diary which has lain there quite ten years,
And soon forget what I am looking for,
Intrigued by cryptic entries in a hand
Resembling mine but noticeably more
Vigorous than my present quavering scrawl.
Appointments—kept or not, I don't remember—
With people now grown narrow, fat or bald;
A list of books that somehow I have never
Found the time to read, nor ever shall,
Remind me that my world is growing cold.
And then I find a scribbled code and number,
The urgent words: 'Must not forget to call.'
But now, of course, I have no recollection
Of telephoning anyone at all.
The questions whisper: Did I dial that number
And, if I did, what kind of voice replied?
Questions that will never find an answer
Unless—the thought is serpentine—I tried
To telephone again, as years ago
I did, or meant to do. What would I find

If now I lifted this mechanic slave
Black to my ear and spun the dial—so . . .?
Inhuman, impolite, the double burp
Erupts, insulting hope. The long dark sleeve
Of silence stretches out. No stranger's voice
Slips in, suspicious, cold; no manic speech
Telling what I do not wish to know
Nor throaty message creamed with sensual greed—
Nothing of these. And, when again I try,
Relief is painful when there's no reply.

Felo de Se

Alone, he came to his decision,
The sore tears stiffening his cheeks
As headlamps flicked the ceiling with white dusters
And darkness roared downhill with nervous brakes.
Below, the murmuring and laughter,
The baritone, tobacco-smelling jokes;
And then his misery and anger
Suddenly became articulate:
'I wish that I was dead. Oh, they'll be sorry then.
I hate them and I'll kill myself tomorrow.
I want to die. I hate them, hate them. Hate.'

And kill himself in fact he did,
But not next day as he'd decided.
The deed itself, for thirty years deferred,
Occurred one wintry night when he was loaded.
Belching with scotch and misery
He turned the gas tap on and placed his head
Gently, like a pudding, in the oven.
'I want to die. I'll hurt them yet,' he said.
And once again: 'I hate them, hate them. Hate.'
The lampless darkness roared inside his head,
Then sighed into a silence in which played
The grown-up voices, still up late,
Indifferent to his rage as to his fate.

The Fair

Music and yellow steam, the fizz
Of spinning lights as roundabouts
Galloping nowhere whirl and whizz
Through fusillades of squeals and shouts;
The night sniffs rich at pungent spice,
Brandysnap and diesel oil;
The stars like scattered beads of rice
Sparsely fleck the sky's deep soil
Dulled and diminished by these trapped
Melodic meteors below
In whose feigned fever brightly lapped
The innocent excitements flow.
Pocketfuls of simple thrills
Jingle silver, purchasing
A warm and sugared fear that spills
From dizzy car and breathless swing.

So no one hears the honest shriek
From the field beyond the fair,
A single voice becoming weak,
Then dying on the ignorant air.
And not for hours will frightened love
Rise and seek her everywhere,
Then find her, like a fallen glove,
Soiled and crumpled, lying there.

Dead Dog

One day I found a lost dog in the street.
The hairs about its grin were spiked with blood,
And it lay still as stone. It must have been
A little dog, for though I only stood
Nine inches for each one of my four years
I picked it up and took it home. My mother

Squealed, and later father spaded out
A bed and tucked my mongrel down in mud.

I can't remember any feeling but
A moderate pity, cool not swollen-eyed;
Almost a godlike feeling now it seems.
My lump of dog was ordinary as bread.
I have no recollection of the school
Where I was taught my terror of the dead.

Autobiographical Note

Beeston, the place, near Nottingham:
We lived there for three years or so.
Each Saturday at two-o'clock
We queued up for the matinée,
All the kids for streets around
With snotty noses, giant caps,
Cut down coats and heavy boots,
The natural enemies of cops
And schoolteachers. Profane and hoarse
We scrambled, yelled and fought until
The Picture Palace opened up
And we, like Hamelin children, forced
Our bony way into the hall.
That much is easy to recall;
Also the reek of chewing-gum,
Gob-stoppers and liquorice,
But of the flickering myths themselves
Not much remains. The hero was
A milky wide-brimmed hat, a shape
Astride the arched white stallion;
The villain's horse and hat were black.
Disbelief did not exist
And laundered virtue always won
With quicker gun and harder fist,
And all of us applauded it.

Yet I remember moments when
In solitude I'd find myself
Brooding on the sooty man,
The bristling villain, who could move
Imagination in a way
The well-shaved hero never could,
And even warm the nervous heart
With something oddly close to love.

The Great War

Whenever war is spoken of
I find
The war that was called Great invades the mind:
The grey militia marches over land
A darker mood of grey
Where fractured tree-trunks stand
And shells, exploding, open sudden fans
Of smoke and earth.
Blind murders scythe
The deathscape where the iron brambles writhe;
The sky at night
Is honoured with rosettes of fire,
Flares that define the corpses on the wire
As terror ticks on wrists at zero hour.
These things I see,
But they are only part
Of what it is that slyly probes the heart:
Less vivid images and words excite
The sensuous memory
And, even as I write,
Fear and a kind of love collaborate
To call each simple conscript up
For quick inspection:
Trenches' parapets
Paunchy with sandbags; bandoliers, tin-hats,
Candles in dug-outs,

Duckboards, mud and rats.
Then, like patrols, tunes creep into the mind:
A long long trail The Rose of No-Man's Land,
Home Fires and *Tipperary*;
And through the misty keening of a band
Of Scottish pipes the proper names are heard
Like fateful commentary of distant guns:
Passchendaele, Bapaume, and Loos, and Mons.
And now,
Whenever the November sky
Quivers with a bugle's hoarse, sweet cry,
The reason darkens; in its evening gleam
Crosses and flares, tormented wire, grey earth
Splattered with crimson flowers,
And I remember,
Not the war I fought in
But the one called Great
Which ended in a sepia November
Four years before my birth.

The Men Who Wear My Clothes

Sleepless I lay last night and watched the slow
   Procession of the men who wear my clothes:
First, the grey man with bloodshot eyes and sly
   Gestures miming what he loves and loathes.

Next came the cheery knocker-back of pints,
   The beery joker, never far from tears,
Whose loud and public vanity acquaints
   The careful watcher with his private fears.

And then I saw the neat mouthed gentle man
   Defer politely, listen to the lies,
Smile at the tedious tale and gaze upon
   The little mirrors in the speaker's eyes.

The men who wear my clothes walked past my bed
    And all of them looked tired and rather old;
I felt a chip of ice melt in my blood.
    Naked I lay last night, and very cold.

Juan in Middle Age

The appetite which leads him to her bed
Is not unlike the lust of boys for cake
Except he knows that after he has fed
He'll suffer more than simple belly-ache.

He'll groan to think what others have to pay
As price for his obsessive need to know
That he's a champion still, though slightly grey,
And both his skill and gameness clearly show.

And after this quick non-decision bout,
As he in his dark corner gasping lies,
He'll hear derision like a distant shout
While kisses press like pennies on his eyes.

Incident in a Saloon Bar

Not because he was in any way remarkable
In dress, physique, or conjunction of facial parts
Did the rest of the customers feel such embarrassment
And curious fear in their superstitious hearts.

That all of them, to some degree, were so afflicted
Was evident from the way their lips grew tight,
And from the intensity with which they did not stare at him,
Though each could have stated his colouring and height.

Not because he was conspicuously intoxicated
Or publishing uncouth sounds or venereal signs
Did his presence so patently offend those stiff gentlemen
Who, guardsmen of propriety, presented him their spines.

Not because he was so quiet and unremarkable
That they suspected that he might be spying
Did they feel this hostility towards the lonely fellow
But simply because he was, quite quietly, crying.

Wedding

The white flower of his love grew in the shade
Of cypress and was nourished by forlorn
And haunting arias of birds afraid
Of that bright dark, the clarion murderous dawn.

The moon, diseased and beautiful, approved his choice
Of meadow saffron, wolf's-bane and the icy blade
He gave to her he loved. At last her voice
Whispered the consent for which he prayed.

But she insisted on a long engagement,
And well before the wedding day drew near
He found out what the darkening cage of age meant;
His sugared love changed into acid fear.

The date could not be cancelled, but instead
Of coloured paper snow the salt rain fell,
And he, pale groom, lay blind in her deep bed,
Ears stopped against the tolling of the bell.

Elegy

The world burst (*plap!*) like a black balloon
In a black room:

Black silence, a black moon.
This occurred on a summer afternoon
In the year 1959 on July the 3rd.

The enormous nostrils of everywhere
Were pinched tight, hard;
Blind to reek, stench and sweet rumour,
To laborious sweat,
And deaf to the aria of the rose.

Music knifed in a flash
Daggered at that *plap*!

Ridiculous. And ridiculous too
That all the wild wide women then were sealed,
Stopped, blocked and chilled
When my old friend, the boozer Bellamy, expired
As, I suppose, in that same tick of time
And equally absurdly
Five hundred thousand other worlds misfired,
Speaking statistically.

Dejection

Not worthy of the fine words, this sensation—
Despair, deep-eyed may mouth its rich iambics,
Betrayal's tears move softly and in tune—
To dignify this with the name of torment
Would only puff it up, a toy balloon,
And make its owner clownish and a liar.

No dark night of the soul, but afternoon,
Quite dark it's true, and grizzled with chill rain;
The whole terrain a wintry cabbage patch;
Some stale confetti trodden in the mud.
I seek the words and images that match
The dun, the moribund, the colour of this mood,
And now intone these lines at sombre pitch,
Accompanied by one distressed bassoon.

Howling for Love

Howling for love in his unfriendly bed
At length he slept, grew muscles in his dream,
And thrashed the hairy villain with his father's face,
And kissed the woman on her tubs of cream.

The soft explosion of the sunrise flung
Him gasping in the whistling world; derisions peeped
And sniggered on the windowsill;
Through sticky lashes wincing daylight seeped.

The clanging challenge of the day began.
The shawl of sun was warm as auburn breath;
The tinkling walk of women told him love;
Dumb music churned his blood to crimson wealth.

Evening was moondrenched when he met his love;
Her breasts were smooth as peeled eggs, and she lay
Her white, unplundered beauty at his wish
And prayed that he would hold the dawn at bay.

But even as he sank into her cry
He knew betrayal curled on her dark head,
And moaned that he had never wanted this,
Howling for love in his unfriendly bed.

Cows in Red Pasture

Last summer in a Kentish field
I saw the plush green darkened by
A whim of light and darkened too
By whiteness of the sheep which stood
Diminished by the distance so
They looked like gravestones on the green,
So still and small and white they seemed.

As this warm memory blurs and fades,
The emptiness bequeathed instructs
Me, curiously, to resurrect
An older memory of a field
Which I would rather far forget:
A foreign field, a field of France,
In which there lay two cows, one white
With maps of black stamped on its hide,
The other just the colour of
The caramel that I once loved.
Both were still; the toffee one
Lay on its back, its stiff legs stuck
Up from the swollen belly like
A huge discarded set of bagpipes.
The piebald cow lay on its side
Looking like any summer beast
Until one saw it had no head.

The grass on which they lay was red.

A Day on the River

It moved so slowly, friendly as a dog
Whose teeth would never bite;
It licked the hand with cool and gentle tongue
And seemed to share its parasites' delight
Who moved upon its back or moored among
The hairy shallows overhung
With natural parasols of leaves
And bubbling birdsong.
Ukuleles twanged and ladies sang
In punts and houseboats vivid as our own
Bold paintings of the Ark;
This was summer's self to any child:
The plop and suck of water and the old
Sweet rankness in the air beguiled

With deft archaic spells the dim
Deliberations of the land,
Dear river, comforting
More than the trailing hand.

The afternoon of sandwiches and flasks
Drifted away.
The breeze across the shivering water grew
Perceptibly in strength. The sun began to bleed.

'Time to go home,' the punctured uncles said,
And back on land
We trembled at the river's faint, low growl
And as birds probed the mutilated sky
We knew that, with the night,
The river's teeth grew sharp
And they could bite.

The Wicked Words

The wicked words corrupt. The young are gorged
On printed sex and violence till they tear
The pages up, still grunting with the urge
To rip a softer substance. Everywhere
The literate werewolves roam in drooling quest
Of nice white meat. Dread walks on pointed toes.
The wicked words corrupt, should be suppressed.
The young men tick like bombs in darkened bars,
Swallow the scalding music, pupils glow
Like fuses, dangerous. Yes, I suppose
They are quite capable of violent acts,
Translating into deed the feverish prose.
The odd thing is I've never seen them read,
Not wicked words nor any words at all,
As I've seen wrinkled gents and wispy dames
Munching up the print with serious greed,
The print recording deeds of lust and terror,

Incest, murder, rape and God knows what,
Intrepid readers who would squeak with horror
To see a mouse or dog or pussy bleed
And vomit at the sight of human snot.

A Sordid Story

All the dark watchers trembled when they saw
The lovers who, as they lay down together
In desperate conjunction, also raped
Convention and made decent dewlaps shudder.

Above the town, on Beacon Hill, the rain
Homed in her hair as sweetly as on leaves,
And when he sank inside her welcoming,
'Home!' he exulted, there beneath drenched trees.

But in the town the files were being opened;
A ginger man who smelled of nicotine,
Who'd never heard of Paolo or Francesca,
Was filling in the date and place and time.

Her body made all similes of need
Die in the throat; itself was metaphor,
For, though it was substantial as good bread,
Its language was alive as no words are.

And neither tried to turn the flesh to words;
They dared not challenge time with hollow nouns
Or truss the moment with syllabic cords
However neat: no page would print their groans.

No, not their groans but fact and circumstance,
Blurred pictures of the pair, a trull and clown:
A sordid story in smudged type it danced,
Blown through the midnight gutters of the town.

My Father's Face

Each morning, when I shave, I see his face,
Or something like a sketch of it gone wrong;
The artist caught, it seems, more than a trace
Of that uneasy boldness and the strong
Fear behind the stare which tried to shout
How tough its owner was, inviting doubt.

And though this face is altogether
Loosely put together, and indeed
A lot less handsome, weaker in the jaw
And softer in the mouth, I feel no need
To have it reassembled, made a better
Copy of the face of its begetter.

I do not mind because my mouth is not
That lipless hyphen, military, stern;
He had the face that faces blade and shot
In schoolboys' tales, and even schoolboys learn
To laugh at it. But they've not heard it speak
Those bayonet words that guard the cruel and weak.

For weakness was his one consistency;
And when I scrape the soapy fluff away
I see that he bequeathed this gift to me
Along with various debts I cannot pay.
But he gave, too, this mirror-misting breath
Whose mercy dims the looking-glass of death;

For which kind accident I thank him now
And, though I cannot love him, feel a sort
Of salty tenderness, remembering how
The prude and lecher in him moiled and fought
Their roughhouse in the dark ring of his pride
And killed each other when his body died.

This morning, as I shave, I find I can
Forgive the blows, the meanness and the lust,

The ricochetting arsenal of a man
Who groaned groin-deep in hope's ironic dust;
But these eyes in the glass regard the living
Features with distaste, quite unforgiving.

An Old Lament Renewed

The soil is savoury with their bones' lost marrow;
  Down among dark roots their polished knuckles lie,
And no one could tell one peeled head from another;
  Earth packs each crater that once gleamed with eye.

Colonel and batman, emperor and assassin,
  Democratized by silence and corruption,
Defy identification with identical grin:
  The joke is long, will brook no interruption.

At night the imagination walks like a ghoul
  Among the stone lozenges and counterpanes of turf
Tumescent under cypresses; the long, rueful call
  Of the owl soars high and then wheels back to earth.

And brooding over the enormous dormitory
  The mind grows shrill at those nothings in lead rooms
Who were beautiful once or dull and ordinary,
  But loved, all loved, all called to sheltering arms.

Many I grieve with a grave, deep love
  Who are deep in the grave, whose faces I never saw:
Poets who died of alcohol, bullets, or birthdays
  Doss in the damp house, forbidden now to snore.

And in a French orchard lies whatever is left
  Of my friend, Gordon Rennie, whose courage would toughen
The muscle of resolution; he laughed
  At death's serious face, but once too often.

On summer evenings when the religious sun stains
  The gloom in the bar and the glasses surrender demurely
I think of Donovan whose surrender was unconditional,
  That great thirst swallowed entirely.

And often some small thing will summon the memory
  Of my small son, Benjamin. A smile is his sweet ghost.
But behind, in the dark, the white twigs of his bones
  Form a pattern of guilt and waste.

I am in mourning for the dull, the heroic and the mad;
  In the haunted nursery the child lies dead.
I mourn the hangman and his bulging complement;
  I mourn the cadaver in the egg.

The one-eyed rider aims, shoots death into the womb;
  Blood on the sheet of snow, the maiden dead.
The dagger has a double blade and meaning,
  So has the double bed.

Imagination swaggers in the sensual sun
  But night will find it at the usual mossy gate;
The whisper from the mouldering darkness comes:
  'I am the one you love and fear and hate.'

I know my grieving is made thick by terror;
  The bones of those I loved aren't fleshed by sorrow.
I mourn the deaths I've died and go on dying;
  I fear the long, implacable tomorrow.

WALKING WOUNDED
1965

Autumn

It is the football season once more
And the back pages of the Sunday papers
Again show the blurred anguish of goalkeepers.

In Maida Vale, Golders Green and Hampstead
Lamps ripen early in the surprising dusk;
They are furred like stale rinds with a fuzz of mist.

The pavements of Kensington are greasy;
The wind smells of burnt porridge in Bayswater,
And the leaves are mushed to silence in the gutter.

The big hotel like an anchored liner
Rides near the park; lit windows hammer the sky.
Like the slow swish of surf the tyres of taxis sigh.

On Ealing Broadway the cinema glows
Warm behind glass while mellow the church clock chimes
As the waiting girls stir in their delicate chains.

Their eyes are polished by the wind,
But the gleam is dumb, empty of joy or anger.
Though the lovers are long in coming the girls still linger.

We are nearing the end of the year.
Under the sombre sleeve the blood ticks faster
And in the dark ear of Autumn quick voices whisper.

It is a time of year that's to my taste,
Full of spiced rumours, sharp and velutinous flavours,
Dim with the mist that softens the cruel surfaces,
Makes mirrors vague. It is the mist that I most favour.

Talking of Death

My friend was dead. A simple sentence ended
With one black stop, like this: My friend was dead.
I had no notion that I had depended
So much on fires he lit, on that good bread
He always had to offer if I came
Hungry and cold to his inviting room.
Absurdly, I believed that he was lame
Until I started limping from his tomb.
My sorrow was the swollen, prickly kind,
Not handsome mourning smartly cut and pressed:
An actual grief, I swear. Therefore to find
Myself engaged upon a shameful quest
For anyone who'd known him, but who thought
That he was still alive, was something strange,
Something disquieting; for what I sought
Was power and presence beyond my usual range.
For once, my audience listened, welcomed me,
Avid for every syllable that spoke
Of woven fear and grieving. Nervously
They eyed my black, ambassadorial cloak.
Their faces greyed; my friend's death died, and they
Saw theirs walk in alive. I felt quite well—
Being Death's man—until they went away,
And I was left with no one else to tell.

Act of Love

This is not the man that women choose,
This honest fellow, stuffed to the lips with groans,
Whose passion cannot even speak plain prose
But grunts and mumbles in the muddiest tones.
His antics are disgusting or absurd,
His lust obtrusive, craning from its nest
At awkward times its blind reptilian head;
His jealousy and candour are a pest.

Now here is the boy that women will lie down for,
The snappy actor, skilled in the lover's part,
A lyric fibber and subvocal tenor
Whose pleasure in the play conceals his art;
Who, even as he enters her warm yes,
Hears fluttering hands and programmes in the vast
Auditorium beyond her voice
Applauding just one member of the cast.

Telephoning Her

The dial spins back, clicks still. Just half an inch
Of silence, then the abrupt eruption blurts
Its two quick jets of noise into his ear.
Again the double spurt; again. Three, four.
She does not answer. Give her just two more.
Yet still he holds the instrument to his ear,
But no longer is imagination bare.
Inside his head the room assumes its shape:
The dishevelled bed, a stocking on the floor.
The tortured clown grimaces in his frame;
The room seems empty, but how can he be sure?
And with uncertainty the light grows dim,.
But not before he sees a movement there,
Quick twitching of the coverings on the bed,
Or thinks he might have noticed something stir.
Darkness grows thick as tar. Then he can hear—
Though not in the liquorice-black thing that he holds—
Her voice, thick with the body's joy and mind's despair,
Moaning a foreign word, a stranger's name.
Derisively the darkness jerks again,
Spits twice into his violated ear.

It's Sure to End in Tears

'It's sure to end in tears.
These rough games always do.
Come downstairs! Where's that book
That Auntie Georgie gave you?
Get your crayons, make a picture.
Stay apart. Don't touch.
You know as well as I what happens
When your games start getting rough.
Now don't get so excited dears
Or everything will end in tears,'

And she was right. Things always did:
Wild giggle in mid-air would flip
A sudden somersault and turn
To yell of pain. The dizzy branch
Of fun would crack; a shrill swoop down,
Black flash of bump, and pain began;
Or, more insidious than pain,
Excitement's swing came lurching low
To darkened ground where nothing grew
And all the air was sick and stale.
The best games always ended so,
With pain or boredom, screams and jeers;
Were always sure to end in tears.

So let us, Love, be circumspect,
For we are wiser than we were;
We are not children and must act
With pressed decorum, keeping far
Apart on couches, stay downstairs,
Read serious books, play nothing rough;
And if, at times, caught unawares,
We think of those hot games and laugh,
Perhaps, in folly, wish once more
To swing branch high, roll on the floor,

We'll summon that calm voice which said,
'It's sure to end in tears' and go
Sober to our separate beds
Where, should we weep, no one will know.

Voyeur

Find the hidden face. A prize is offered.
The scene is green and summer. On the grass
The dresses spread, exhausted butterflies,
And smooth brown legs make soft confessions to
Rough trousers. Excited air
Is hushed with kissing.
Now search for the solitary, the uncoupled one:
Not in the leafy tentacles of trees,
He is no climber,
But close to earth, well-hidden, squat.
You see him now? Yes, there! His snarling grin
Bearded with leaves, his body bushed,
Invisible. See how his eyes are fat with glee
And horror. They fizz with unfulfilment's booze.
His tongue makes sure his lips are still in place
With quick red pats.
You've found him now, and you can take your prize,
Though, as you see, we do not offer cash:
Just recognition and its loaded cosh.

Walking Wounded

A mammoth morning moved grey flanks and groaned.
In the rusty hedges pale rags of mist hung;
The gruel of mud and leaves in the mauled lane
Smelled sweet, like blood. Birds had died or flown,

Their green and silent attics sprouting now
With branches of leafed steel, hiding round eyes
And ripe grenades ready to drop and burst.
In the ditch at the cross-roads the fallen rider lay
Hugging his dead machine and did not stir
At crunch of mortar, tantrum of a Bren
Answering a Spandau's manic jabber.
Then into sight the ambulances came,
Stumbling and churning past the broken farm,
The amputated sign-post and smashed trees,
Slow wagonloads of bandaged cries, square trucks
That rolled on ominous wheels, vehicles
Made mythopoeic by their mortal freight
And crimson crosses on the dirty white.
This grave procession passed, though, for a while,
The grinding of their engines could be heard,
A dark noise on the pallor of the morning,
Dark as dried blood; and then it faded, died.
The road was empty, but it seemed to wait—
Like a stage which knows the cast is in the wings—
Wait for a different traffic to appear.
The mist still hung in snags from dripping thorns;
Absent-minded guns still sighed and thumped.
And then they came, the walking wounded,
Straggling the road like convicts loosely chained,
Dragging at ankles exhaustion and despair.
Their heads were weighted down by last night's lead,
And eyes still drank the dark. They trailed the night
Along the morning road. Some limped on sticks;
Others wore rough dressings, splints and slings;
A few had turbanned heads, the dirty cloth
Brown-badged with blood. A humble brotherhood,
Not one was suffering from a lethal hurt,
They were not magnified by noble wounds,
There was no splendour in that company.
And yet, remembering after eighteen years,
In the heart's throat a sour sadness stirs;
Imagination pauses and returns
To see them walking still, but multiplied
In thousands now. And when heroic corpses

Turn slowly in their decorated sleep
And every ambulance has disappeared
The walking wounded still trudge down that lane,
And when recalled they must bear arms again.

A Case of Murder

They should not have left him there alone,
Alone that is except for the cat.
He was only nine, not old enough
To be left alone in a basement flat,
Alone, that is, except for the cat.
A dog would have been a different thing,
A big gruff dog with slashing jaws,
But a cat with round eyes mad as gold,
Plump as a cushion with tucked-in paws—
Better have left him with a fair-sized rat!
But what they did was leave him with a cat.
He hated that cat; he watched it sit,
A buzzing machine of soft black stuff,
He sat and watched and he hated it,
Snug in its fur, hot blood in a muff,
And its mad gold stare and the way it sat
Crooning dark warmth: he loathed all that.
So he took Daddy's stick and he hit the cat.
Then quick as a sudden crack in glass
It hissed, black flash, to a hiding place
In the dust and dark beneath the couch,
And he followed the grin on his new-made face,
A wide-eyed, frightened snarl of a grin,
And he took the stick and he thrust it in,
Hard and quick in the furry dark.
The black fur squealed and he felt his skin
Prickle with sparks of dry delight.
Then the cat again came into sight,
Shot for the door that wasn't quite shut,

But the boy, quick too, slammed fast the door:
The cat, half-through, was cracked like a nut
And the soft black thud was dumped on the floor.
Then the boy was suddenly terrified
And he bit his knuckles and cried and cried;
But he had to do something with the dead thing there.
His eyes squeezed beads of salty prayer
But the wound of fear gaped wide and raw;
He dared not touch the thing with his hands
So he fetched a spade and shovelled it
And dumped the load of heavy fur
In the spidery cupboard under the stair
Where it's been for years, and though it died
It's grown in that cupboard and its hot low purr
Grows slowly louder year by year:
There'll not be a corner for the boy to hide
When the cupboard swells and all sides split
And the huge black cat pads out of it.

Hide and Seek

Call out. Call loud: 'I'm ready! Come and find me!'
The sacks in the toolshed smell like the seaside.
They'll never find you in this salty dark,
But be careful that your feet aren't sticking out.
Wiser not to risk another shout.
The floor is cold. They'll probably be searching
The bushes near the swing. Whatever happens
You mustn't sneeze when they come prowling in.
And here they are, whispering at the door;
You've never heard them sound so hushed before.
Don't breathe. Don't move. Stay dumb. Hide in your
                                 blindness.
They're moving closer, comeone stumbles, mutters;
Their words and laughter scuffle, and they're gone.
But don't come out just yet; they'll try the lane
And then the greenhouse and back here again.

They must be thinking that you're very clever,
Getting more puzzled as they search all over.
It seems a long time since they went away.
Your legs are stiff, the cold bites through your coat;
The dark damp smell of sand moves in your throat.
It's time to let them know that you're the winner.
Push off the sacks. Uncurl and stretch. That's better!
Out of the shed and call to them: 'I've won!
Here I am! Come and own up I've caught you!'
The darkening garden watches. Nothing stirs.
The bushes hold their breath; the sun is gone.
Yes, here you are. But where are they who sought you?

Unacademic Graffiti

The coin slips down with a metallic gulp;
The door submits, steps back, slams shut again.
Buttocks are bared; the seat is slightly warm,
Distasteful relic of a former reign.
The cell is small and mainly functional,
Yet something more: this privacy is rare,
Perhaps unique, self-conscious, quintessential.
This, and of course the business why we're here,
May be the reason why the mental bowels
Move to expel dark cargo of their own.
There, on the door and on the gaolish walls
Are aspirations that we can't disown:
The chronic thirst for immortality,
Someone's name carved by a penknife blade,
Not ours of course though it might easily be
Were we not quite so prudent or afraid;
And we, too, might have drawn those zeppelin cocks,
Ballooning balls and ladies on their backs
With wide flung legs revealing beetling twats
Had we not often felt the punch guilt packs.
And we feel solitude encouraging
Confessions that no penitent would make;

The words upon the walls are whispering
Our loneliness and lust, despair and hate.
We notice, unsurprised and unappalled,
That someone's done an abstract with his shit.
It's time to go. Heave off. The chain is pulled.
Gurgle and gush. Outside the lamps are lit
But in the padlocked park the night is thick;
Down baffled alleys desperations sob;
In blinded upper rooms the air is sick,
And everywhere the human engines throb.

Report on Drinking Habits

I

He is always well-shaven; often
His jowl is powdered like something
Carefully prepared for the oven.
He is plump but not corpulent.
It is talk he wants rather than drinking,
Though nowhere else than in a saloon
Could he find the conversation
He needs, metallic as a spittoon,
Masculine as beef and mustard.
He always buys a round before leaving
But never stays for more than half an hour
And two or three drinks, and no one
Has ever observed him hungover.
His eyes' brightness advertises
Good meals and unadventurous sleeping.

II

This one is a different case: he starts
Fast, towsing his glass like a dog
With bone, welcomes it when the drink hurts
Exploding in dark diaphragm.

The presiding clock watches his knees sag.
He is not much interested in talk
And the most he will ever eat
Is a sandwich, or sausage on stick;
He is sometimes accompanied
By a mournful woman who does not speak.
Three hours produce a visible change:
His eyes smear and his face grows fat,
A dredged cadaver's except for the tinge
Of diseased sunset through the sweat.
Closing time strikes like a fatal attack.

III

But for this other one drink is not
A murderous necessity,
A vice or pleasant social habit;
For him it is a vocation.
Virtue is no more than capacity.
He will talk because, by speaking, he
Can show that he is capable.
If you meet him in the lavatory
He will remark on the weather,
But his words are never memorable.
Like a professional athlete he
Paces himself and finishes
Strongly. Nobody will ever see
Him collapse or even falter.
At the last bell he quietly vanishes.

IV

Watch the next customer; observe him
Grabbing with eyes and mouth and fist.
He likes to talk, also, as the rim
Of gripped glass trembles to get in,
Promises to be better than the last.
Gay joker early in the evening,
Later a mournful bulldozer
Incorrigibly revealing
Public parts he believes are secret;

From the opening bell a certain loser.
In the morning it will be never
Again, never to be realized.
Observe this fellow in the mirror:
The daft mask mocks all promises,
Sticks fast and hurts, and must be recognized.

Mourning

We sat in the kitchen and listened to the rain
That spluttered on the pane like something frying.
The silence simmered but we did not season it;
We had mislaid effective flavouring.
Each of us knew the other's heart was tight,
Swollen and taut, like something overripe;
But neither spilled a drop of salty water.
I do not know how long we stayed like that,
An hour, at least, for the room was growing dark
When one of us rose and switched on the light.
Chairs groaned and sighed, and then at last she spoke:
We had to decide what to eat that night.

Revenant

There is a smell of negligence;
Dust pads the evening shadows;
The room has become small.
I remember the bird-shaped stain
Brown on the yellow wall.

This room was once familiar,
In which I move, a stranger;
The window holds a view
Faded like a print;
Even the smell is new,

New, yet also ancient,
And the dusty stuff I finger,
The books I must have read,
One cuff-link, postcards, letters,
Seem things left by the dead.

The room attends my going;
Watchfully it waits
To occupy itself.
My feet move down the stairs,
Noiselessly, with stealth.

Since Donovan Died

Death has been named so many times before,
Its avatar determined by blind needs:
Pale rider, lover, angel, king, slammed door;
Scientific fact or worm that feeds
Under numb earth plumping with pale blood;
As if our naming could propitiate,
Redeem the voices from dumb cells of mud.
I will not flatter Death, conceal my hate,
But name it, yes. Since Donovan died I've felt
Anger like a cinder in my gut,
So dirty was the trick that he was dealt,
Such innocent trust was chosen for a butt.
So I name Death, not proud, of regal stock,
But pale, malevolent; a cruel boy
Who pulls the thin black arms out of the clock,
Burns calendars alive with sniggering joy.

Frankly Speaking: An Interview

'Listeners will be interested to hear
This programme where our greatest man of letters

And possibly the greatest man in any
Sphere of intellectual endeavour
Speaks frankly from the wisdom gathered over
A long and varied life. This mellow store
I'm sure will edify and entertain
Without imposing on us too much strain.
We're speaking from the great man's lovely home
And seated in his splendid book-lined room. . . .'

Eight million listeners act their patient role:
They listen. The sharp young voice begins to probe
With confidence, and then the old one comes,
Dusty and frail. One almost smells the mould
Of yellow pages, but no illumination
Brightens bed-sitter, drawing-room and kitchen.
The notions are banal, the phrasing dull;
The stout words with their double chins wheeze out:
The Absolute, the True, the Beautiful.
Then as time wastes, the mouth begins to utter
Dry syllables that flutter like hurt moths.

Determined not to fail, the interviewer
Affects a brisker tone, a little too
Like a policeman's for this interview:
'Now you, sir, as a most exceptional man
Who's pondered long and deep on what goes on
Upon this earth and in the human heart,
Perhaps you'll tell us now what you believe
About the life to come beyond the grave.'

A silence seems to chill the air and threaten
The listener in his armchair or warm kitchen;
And then the great man speaks, quite clearly now:
'Get out! Get out of here you prying fool!
Let in the white men in their soft black boots
Who come with measuring instruments to prove
I'm no exception to their iron rule.'

This Summer

See the stout man with the bald head
Pink as plastic in the polishing sun
Pause on the threshold emerging from the bank,
Petrified by dazzle.

Heat crumbles the afternoon to dust;
Windscreen and chrome flash desperate messages;
A girl in yellow walks past Woolworths,
Her legs oiled with lust.

And who lingeringly chiselled them,
Those indolent limbs lacquered in oil and gold?
Who but him, and of his making
The lush eatable hair.

The crazed man with the hot bald head,
He made them, stunned with lust and summer
On the steps of the Westminster Bank,
Overdrawn and hopelessly happy.

Six Year Darling

The poets are to blame, or partly so:
Wordsworth's pretty pigmy, plump with joy,
And Henry Vaughan's white celestial thoughts
Mislead as much as Millais' chubby boy
Or daddy-blessing Christopher at prayer.
These fantasies are still quite popular.
Pick up any children's book and you will see
That all the illustrations are as false
As muscle-builders' ads: angelic girls
And sturdy little chaps with candid eyes—
Not to please the children, understand;
You'll find few kids who're kidded by the act,

Though later most of them will take the bribe
And speak of infancy as paradise.
Will this boy, here, be legatee of lies?
Perhaps he will, and maybe just as well
If one day he is going to breed his own.
But now he knows that things are otherwise:
Not paradise, no glimpse of God's bright face,
But time of simple goods like warmth and sweets,
Excitement, too; but often pain and fear,
And worse than either, boredom, long and grey,
A dusty road to nowhere, hard to walk,
Going on and on, desolate and bare,
Until it breaks upon the hidden dark.

I'm Covered Now

'What would happen to your lady wife
And little ones—you've four I think you said—
Little ones I mean, not wives, ha-ha—
What would happen to them if . . .' And here
He cleared his throat of any reticence.
'. . . if something happened to you? We've got to face
These things, must be realistic, don't you think?
Now, we have various schemes to give you cover
And, taking in account your age and means,
This policy would seem to be the one . . .'

The words uncoiled, effortless but urgent,
Assured, yet coming just a bit too fast,
A little breathless, despite the ease of manner,
An athlete drawing near the tape's last gasp
Yet trying hard to seem still vigorous there.
But no, this metaphor has too much muscle;
His was an indoor art and every phrase
Was handled with a trained seducer's care.
I took the words to heart, or, if not heart,
Some region underneath intelligence,

The area where the hot romantic aria
And certain kinds of poetry are received.
And this Giovanni of the fast buck knew
My humming brain was pleasurably numb;
My limbs were weakening; he would soon achieve
The now explicit ends for which he'd come.
At last I nodded, glazed, and said I'd sign,
But he showed little proper satisfaction.
He sighed and sounded almost disappointed,
And I remembered hearing someone say
No Juan really likes an easy lay.
But I'll say this: he covered up quite quickly
And seemed almost as ardent as before
When he pressed my hand and said that he was happy
And hoped that I was, too.
                                    And then the door
Was closed behind him as our deal was closed.
If something happened I was covered now.
Odd that I felt so chilly, so exposed.

A Note for Biographers

Those early chapters are the ones to watch:
It is too cosily assumed that all
That happens to the eminent will clutch
The reader's buttonhole. Where infants crawl
Is much the same for every baby born,
And later, when the subject walks erect
In private park or back street of a town
The difference is much less than you'd expect.
The little master in expensive tweed
And scabby little mister in huge cap
Suck in same air, are laughed at, bored, afraid:
Their joys and terrors more than overlap,
They are identical. When Christopher
Crouched by father's side to sight that deer

The nightmare that he'd long been tensing for
Banged loud, awake, and father saw his fear.
The boy felt terrible, but no more so
Than little Eddie when Mum said she knew
About the Sunday penny meant to go
Dark in the soft religious bag, not to
The shop which sold sweet paper bags of guilt.
When Christopher was given his Hornby Train
His joy was bright as rails; but Eddie felt
As much delight to wear Dad's watch and chain
Although the watch's pulse had given up
And neither fly-blue arm would move again.
All children's lives are very much alike,
So my advice is keep that early stuff
Down to a page or two. Don't try to make
Nostalgia pay: we've all had quite enough.
What captivates and sells, and always will,
Is what we are: vain, snarled up, and sleazy.
No one is really interesting until
To love him has become no longer easy.

Moral Problem

Impartial dark conceals the true relation
And hides his screwed grimace, the eyeless grin;
His wife receives his violent visitation,
With muffled cries of welcome lets him in.
His vehement dream reshapes her body to
The sweet task that he really wants to do.

His brother exiled to a foreign city,
Months from his heart's address, his candid bed,
Writes to his love a letter long and witty
But leaves frustration's vocables unsaid;
But lust and longing urge him like a knife
To buy a whore and dream he's with his wife.

And who commits adultery? I question:
The one whose need invokes the girl next door
And makes his wife a page in his hot fiction,
Or he who loves his wife inside a whore?
The question whimpers, asking to be fed;
Better all round to wring its neck instead.

Millionaire

His public face is not entirely human,
Though whether more or less is hard to say;
A flourish of his gold-nibbed wand will bring
Obsequious flunkeys, each with loaded tray,
All the world's sweetmeats to his peevish tongue.
The ennui of possessions, shrivelled appetite
Have moulded him a mask, austere, remote,
But not the luminous and moony skull
Of the voluntary holy anchorite.

Contemptuous of all sensual bargains offered,
Yet frightened of the chill, ascetic cell,
His dreamed apotheosis of the human
Derided by the silk and gold and skill
Of master craftsmen with the tape and shears
All helpless to conceal that crumpled skin
Dry and heavy over lizard eyes,
Does he suspect, through sweet bluff of cigars,
A faint stink of the reptile house creeps in?

A world ago, one wonders, did he dream,
Hungry in ghetto or industrial slum,
Of nodding beauties, steaks and grand hotels,
Or did the ache for power provide the fuel
That drove the panting engine of ambition,
Fired by a vision, anarchic, beautiful, cruel?
Or fear perhaps? A zany dream of freedom?
Even if he knew he would not tell,

Though at cold lonely moments he might curse
The fortune that has come to own himself
And locked him in its huge expensive purse.
But now his folded face shows no emotion.
The chauffeur parcels up his legs in plaid,
Salutes and soothes the limousine from the kerb,
Smooth as a liner on a lake of oil,
Reticent as a hearse.

The Great Old Men

Imagination will not see them as
Toddlers nor as adolescent boys,
These monumental gentlemen who gaze
Serenely from smooth paper that employs
Our weekly interest and rewards it well
With far catastrophes and framed displays
Of foreign pain and sewers one can't smell.

The great old men have silver hair, and who
Could see it otherwise? Who see it sprout
In shocking red or bootbrush black; believe
Those graven visages could pimple out
In pustules, little swellings that betray
The dark tumescences whose heavings leave
Night smears upon the body of the day?

Their lives are formed like perfect paragraphs
Or sweet equations, rational and calm;
They marry garden ladies or remain
Celibate but tranquil as a psalm,
To die with dignity in careful rooms,
And after death continue to explain
Our dark predicament from tomes and tombs.

I raise plumed admiration; I bow low
To see each grave contemplative, each brave

And venerable explorer of the mind
At last borne slowly to a solemn grave;
But grief is formal: sombre clothes disguise
The heart's composure; though I draw the blind
No salt glass splinters in the heart's cold eyes.

My heart's own heart is gripped, the eyes are smashed
By other lives and deaths; the obdurate boys
Who would not leave the playground till the bell
Tolled black, who would not sacrifice their toys,
Their tales, their rhymes, their wild games by the sea
For any grown-up prize; whose early knell
Rolled under waves, clanged from the gallows tree.

Not old and wise, not silvered and serene,
But flogged by sensual storms and appetites
That no white meat nor violent wine could ease,
Trampled at noon by hooves from thrashing nights,
They put rope chokers on, capsized in gin
Or dived heart first in fanged and slavering seas.
With love I take their orphaned poems in.

Love in Any City

It could have been any city—London, Rome,
Paris, New York, Chicago—any home
For simmering crowds and parks and monoliths
Pocked with a hundred peeping squares, where myths
Proliferate against the darkening sky
In brilliant beads of light or, in the sly
And sweetened shadows, joggle on a screen;
A place where the poor and sick are rarely seen
But covered up like sores, where the air is rich,
Spiced and spiked to aggravate the itch
Of need for what one can't or dare not say.
She seemed the City's child in every way:
No wimpled pretty, stroking her sad lyre,
Impatient for her silver-plated squire,

She couldn't show that soft pre-raphaelite
Hair that syrups smoothly over white
Marmoreal shoulders, neither were her eyes
Those wistful jellies of astounding size;
And yet, though many might not notice it,
Her gaze reflected sympathy and wit
In such a way that it could claim a kind
Of magic that obscurely undermined
His selfish palisades. And though both used
A taut elliptic idiom which refused
A melting welcome to the lyric or
Enraptured paean, by which they set small store,
When streets were hushed, swept bare by the night's smooth
broom,
A meadow breeze swayed cool in the grateful room
In which, like branches on related trees,
They stirred towards each other, touched and clung,
Awed by the haunting music that was sung.

When We Were Married

She took the book from the shelf
And turned the pages slowly.
'I loved this book,' she said,
'When we were married.

'That song that teases silence
Was a favourite of mine;
It did not grow tedious
While we were married.

'I ate some food tonight
But did not relish it.
It was a dish that I enjoyed
When we were married.

'When we were married,' she said,
And her lashes were glistening,
'I felt at home in this house, that bed.'
But the man was not listening.

Taken in Adultery

Shadowed by shades and spied upon by glass
Their search for privacy conducts them here,
With an irony that neither notices,
To a public house; the wrong time of the year
For outdoor games; where, over gin and tonic,
Best bitter and potato crisps, they talk
Without much zest, almost laconic,
Flipping an occasional remark.
Would you guess that they were lovers, this dull pair?
The answer, I suppose, is yes, you would.
Despite her spectacles and faded hair
And his worn look of being someone's Dad
You know that they are having an affair
And neither finds it doing them much good.
Presumably, in one another's eyes,
They must look different from what we see,
Desirable in some way, otherwise
They'd hardly choose to come here, furtively,
And mutter their bleak needs above the mess
Of fag-ends, crumpled cellophane and crumbs,
Their love-feast's litter. Though they might profess
To find great joy together, all that comes
Across to us is tiredness, melancholy.
When they are silent each seems listening;
There must be many voices in the air:
Reproaches, accusations, suffering
That no amount of passion keeps elsewhere.
Imperatives that brought them to this room,
Stiff from the car's back seat, lose urgency;
They start to wonder who's betraying whom,
How it will end, and how did it begin—
The woman taken in adultery
And the man who feels he, too, was taken in.

The Old Books

They were beautiful, the old books, beautiful I tell you.
You've no idea, you young ones with all those machines;
There's no point in telling you; you wouldn't understand.
You wouldn't know what the word beautiful means.
I remember Mr. Archibald—the old man, not his son—
He said to me right out: 'You've got a beautiful hand,
Your books are a pleasure to look at, real works of art.'
You youngsters with your ball-points wouldn't understand.
You should have seen them, my day book, and sales ledger:
The unused lines were always cancelled in red ink.
You wouldn't find better kept books in the City;
But it's no good talking: I know what you all think:
'He's old. He's had it. He's living in the past,
The poor old sod.' Well, I don't want your pity.
My forty-seventh Christmas with the firm. Too much to drink.
You're staring at me, pitying. I can tell by your looks.
You'll never know what it was like, what you've missed.
You'll never know. My God, they were beautiful, the old books.

Tightrope Walker

High on the thrilling strand he dances
Laved in white light. The smudged chalk faces
Blur below. His movements scorn
And fluently insult the law
That lumps us, munching, on our seats,
Avoiding the question that slyly tweaks:
How much do we want to see him fall?
It's no use saying we don't at all.
We all know that we hate his breed.
Prancing the nimble thread he's freed
From what we are and gravity.
And yet we know quite well that he

Started just as we began,
That he, like us, is just a man.
(We don't fall off our seats until
We've drunk too much or are feeling ill.)
But he has trained the common skill,
Trained and practised; now tonight
It flogs our credence as high and white
In the spotlight's talcum he pirouettes,
Lonely, scorning safety nets,
The highly extraordinary man.
But soon, quite softly, boredom starts
Its muffled drilling at our hearts;
A frisson of coughs and shuffles moves
Over the crowd like a wind through leaves.
Our eyes slide down the air and walk
Idly round the tent as talk
Hums on denial's monotone.
It's just as well the act ends soon
Or we would leave, though not stampede,
Leave furtively in twos and threes,
Absence flooding the canvas house
Where he, alone, all unaware
Would go on dancing on the almost air
Till fatigue or error dragged him down,
An ordinary man on ordinary ground.

Peerless Jim Driscoll

I saw Jim Driscoll fight in nineteen ten.
That takes you back a bit. You don't see men
Like Driscoll any more. The breed's died out.
There's no one fit to lace his boots about.
All right son. Have your laugh. You know it all.
You think these mugs today that cuff and maul
Their way through ten or fifteen threes can fight:
They hardly know their left hand from their right.

But Jim, he knew: he never slapped or swung,
His left hand flickered like a cobra's tongue
And when he followed with the old one-two
Black lightning of those fists would dazzle you.
By Jesus he could hit. I've never seen
A sweeter puncher: every blow as clean
As silver. *Peerless Jim* the papers named him,
And yet he never swaggered, never bragged.
I saw him once when he got properly tagged—
A sucker punch from nowhere on the chin—
And he was hurt; but all he did was grin
And nod as if to say, 'I asked for that.'
No one was ever more worth looking at;
Up there beneath the ache of arc-lamps he
Was just like what we'd love our sons to be
Or like those gods you've heard about at school . . .
Well, yes, I'm old; and maybe I'm a fool.
I only saw him once outside the ring
And I admit I found it disappointing.
He looked just—I don't know—just ordinary,
And smaller, too, than what I thought he'd be:
An ordinary man in fact, like you or me.

Time for a Quick One

Noon holds the city back;
Its suburbs are five miles away
Where the baker's cry is greyer than the sky
And drapes itself about the television masts.

Here, alcohol explodes
In secret salvoes, glasses chime.
The stew of noise boils over, spills outside,
Calls hungry volunteers to join the garrison.

A veteran lights a fag.
His face is pigmented with rage,

Flayed raw by booze; both eyes have gone to bed.
A new recruit salutes and takes his life in hand.

Malingerers and old sweats,
Stout corporals and cute subalterns
Shout for reinforcements and more rations.
The smoke cuts harsh at eyes and din thumps louder drums.

Outside, the suburbs start
Their noiseless, disciplined advance.
The city waits with finger firm on trigger.
The fort is now surrounded. Soon closing-time will strike.

After the Fireworks

Back into the light and warmth,
Boots clogged with mud, toes
Welded to wedges of cold flesh,
The children warm their hands on mugs
While, on remembered lawns, the flash
Of fireworks dazzles night;
Sparklers spray and rockets swish,
Soar high and break in falling showers
Of glitter; the bonfire gallivants,
Its lavish flames shimmy, prance,
And lick the straddling guy.
We wait for those great leaves of heat
And broken necklaces of light
To dim and die.
And then the children go to bed.
Tomorrow they will search grey ground
For debris of tonight: the sad
And saturated cardboard stems,
The fallen rocket sticks, the charred
Hubs of catherine-wheels;
Then, having gathered all they've found,

They'll leave them scattered carelessly
For us to clear away.
But now the children are asleep,
And you and I sit silently
And hear, from far off in the night,
The last brave rocket burst and fade.
We taste the darkness in the light,
Reflect that fireworks are not cheap
And ask ourselves uneasily
If, even now, we've fully paid.

My Three Hoboes

In the bullion bar of a bright hotel
I gave three tramps a splendid feed.
Though I was poor I fed them well,
Knowing the acreage of their greed.
All around, the double-chinned,
The thin and plump of various ages,
Lacquered with privilege, golden-skinned
Because they paid the sun good wages,
Laughed and drank and did not see
The scruffy hoboes I'd brought there;
In fact they did not notice me,
But we watched them with our reptile stare,
We watched the blond boys and their trulls
Whose taut instructive favours draped
Hard uniform of bones and skulls;
We eyed the stout papas and gaped
At slender daughters' pulchritude,
But not a glance came back our way
As I provided yet more food
For my rough guests.
                I always pay
When my familiar vagrants come
To these palatial joints with me—
Lust and loathing and the other bum,
Envy, strongest of the three.

Dirty Story

The laughter at the bar rumbles rich,
Masculine as steak. More drink is served.
Tankards clang and tumblers ring;
Dull memories are cuffed and searched,
Together heads are bent, intent, and words
From someone wind the spring of mirth again:
Heard the one about the blonde with worms?
Listen. She was sitting on a gate . . .
And so a verbal art is carried on,
Simple as tales of bunnies, elves and moles,
With vicars, golfers, spinsters and cute dolls,
Rabbis and rissoles, condoms and commodes.
Each fable, rhymed, or plain vernacular job,
Insists upon the funniness of lust,
Betrayal, shame, the belly-shaking joke
Of pain and innocence and wounded love.
Again the laughter thickens, swirls like smoke:
"Oh, very good!" they gasp: "Oh Gawd! oh my!"
They laugh till they begin, almost, to cry.

Ruminant

The leather belly shades the buttercups.
Her horns are the yellow of old piano keys.
Hopelessly the tail flicks at the humming heat;
Flies crawl to the pools of her eyes.
She slowly turns her head and watches me
As I approach: her gaze is a silent moo.
I stop and we swap stares. I smoke. She chews.

How do I view her then? As pastoral furniture,
Solid in the green and fluid summer?
A brooding factory of milk and sausages,
Or something to be chopped to bits and sold

In wounded paper parcels? No, as none of these.
My view is otherwise and infantile,
But it survives my own sour sneers.
It is the anthropomorphic fallacy
Which puts brown speculation in those eyes.
But I am taken in: that gentleness endears,
As do the massive patience and submission
Huge among buttercups and flies.
But, in the end, it is those plushy eyes,
The slow and meditative jaws, that hold
Me to this most untenable of views:
Almost, it seems, she might be contemplating
Composing a long poem about Ted Hughes.

My Pen Has Ink Enough

My pen has ink enough; I'm going to start
A piece of verse, but suddenly my heart
And something in my head jerks in reverse.

I can't go on—I did, with switch in tense,
And here's the bleak, accusing evidence;
I don't know why, or even what I seek.

This thought jabbed hard: how insolent to make
These blurred attempts when Shakespeare, Donne and Blake
Have done what they have done. And yet it tempts,

This longing to make wicks of words, light lamps
However frail and dim. And, hell, why not?
I've had six children yet more casually got.

EPITHETS OF WAR
1965

Epithets of War

I

August 1914

The bronze sun blew a long and shimmering call
Over the waves of Brighton and Southend,
Over slapped and patted pyramids of sand,
Paper Union Jacks and cockle stalls;
A pierrot aimed his banjo at the gulls;
Small spades dug trenches to let the channel in
As nimble donkeys followed their huge heads
And charged. In the navy sky the loud white birds
Lolled on no wind, then, swinging breathless, skimmed
The somersaulting waves; a military band
Thumped and brayed, brass pump of sentiment;
And far from the beach, inland, lace curtains stirred.
A girl played Chopin while her sister pored
Over her careful sewing; faint green scent
Of grass was sharpened by a gleam of mint,
And, farther off, in London, horses pulled
Their rumbling drays and vans along the Strand
Or trundled down High Holborn and beyond
The Stadium Club, where, in the wounded world
Of five years later, Georges Carpentier felled
Bulldog Joe Beckett in a single round.
And all is history; its pages smell
Faintly of camphor and dead pimpernel
Coffined in leaves, and something of the sand
And salt of holiday. But dead. The end
Of something never to be lived again.

II

The Guns

A few were preserved years after they had died,
Kept in hushed museums as stuffed animals are;
One, a trench mortar, rested amiably inside
The recreation ground of a midland spa.

The kids took no more notice of it than
The parched fountain or the grass on which they ran.

They were too young to have heard the gun's enormous tongue,
Though the blind voice still broke their parents' sleep:
Black sacks of spilled thunder avalanched among
The pastures of dreamed peace; again pacific sheep
Were slaughtered in hot laughter's howl and boom;
Wraiths of dead cordite smelled sweet in the waking room.

Dawn tamed the darkness in the skull, put thunder down.
Rain slanted hair-thin through the haggard sky;
Again gun-carriages rumbled through the broken town;
Capes gleamed, dark metal, as the infantry marched by.
The guns were silent, but their speakings echoed still:
Anger of names—Cambrai, Bethune, Arras, Kemmel Hill.

Night will surge back, sure as a counter-attack;
Lewis-guns and Vickers will chatter in their fever;
Again the big guns will slam and slash and hack
At silence till it folds about their heads forever;
Then even the names will fade, mere sounds, unbroken code,
Marks on the page: Passchendaele, Verdun, The Menin Road.

III

Casualties

They were printed daily in the newspapers.
A woman in Nottingham went mad reading them;
She drowned herself in the Trent.
Her name was not included in the casualty lists.

She was mother of two million sons.
At night a frail voice would quaver,
Cry from its bed of mud:
'Stretcher-bearers! Stretcher-bearers!' She could not go.

She could not bear it. Her mind broke.
Barbed-wire scrawled illiterate history
Over the black dough of Belgian fields,
Was punctuated by anatomies.

In Trafalgar Square an English lady
Distributed white feathers among civilians.
Children with sad moustaches and puttee'd calves
Prepared to be translated.

The crazed mother heard them at night
Crying as hot stars exploded
And the earth's belly shook and rumbled
With giant eructations.

The ambulances lurched through the mire in the brain;
Uniformed surgeons in crimson aprons
Laboured at irreparable bodies;
Dawn bristled on their skullish jaws.

And two million of an innocent generation,
Orphaned by a doomed, demented mother,
Unlearned an axiom: they discovered
Only the lucky few meet death once only.

IV

War Songs

A lesson that their children knew by heart
Where it lay stonily in that September.
Conscripted man, anonymous in hot
Brown or blue, intoned his rank and number.
The discs, strung from his neck, no amulet
Against the ache of loss, were worn in darkness
Under grave blankets in the narrow cot
After the bugle's skirmish with night's silence.
In trembling cities civil sleep was probed
By the wild sirens' blind and wounded howling;
White searchlights hosed the sky; black planets throbbed;
At night all buildings put on total mourning.
And, when dawn yawned, the washed skies were afloat
With silver saveloys whose idle motion
And conference with puffed clouds appeared to mock
Bereaving night and morning's lamentation.

And then, down country lanes, the crop-haired sons
And nephews of the skeletons of Flanders
Made seance of their march, as, on their tongues,
The old ghosts sang again of Tipperary,
Packing kit-bags, getting back to Blighty,
But soon, bewildered, sank back to their graves
When others songs were bawled—a jaunty music
With false, bragging words: The Siegfried Line
Transformed with comic washing hanging from it,
Sergeants and Corporals were blessed, the barrel rolled;
But behind the grinning words and steady tramping
The Sergeant of the dark was taking names
And marking time to that lugubrious singing.
We're saying goodbye to them all: and, far away
From gunpit, barrack square and trench, the mother
Sewed the dark garments for tomorrow's mourning.

V

Eidolon Parade

A grey wind prowls across the lake of stone,
The flag flicks like a summer horse's tail,
The brass voice of the bugle climbs and clings
High before it crumbles, falls and fades.
C.S.M. Hardy, back from Salerno Beach,
Glitters with sea salt, winkles nest in his eyes,
But his voice grinds loud as ever as he calls
The Nominal Roll: Corporal Mick McGuire
Has returned from Alamein, each orifice
Is clogged with sand; but tonight he will appear
Once more at the Church Hall, battle-dress pressed
And patent leather highlights on his feet;
And when the lights are dimmed, the last waltz makes
Its passionate interrogation: *Who's
Taking You Home Tonight?* who but McGuire,
Although his terrible kiss will taste of sand
Gritting on shocked teeth, and his cold cheek
Will seem to her a stony reprimand.
And, while the Corporal tangoes, Private Bain,
A bunch of quarrels hanging from each wrist,

Will sluice his guts with twenty black-and-tans;
But he stands still now, sober, at attention
With that small company paraded there
Waiting for inspection: Dodger Rae,
Equipment scruffy and an idle bootlace,
Is put on an eternal two-five-two;
Spike Liston, gaunt as a Belsen boy or saint,
Still rages for more grub; Bull Evans broods
On all the thighs he'll never lie between
Or lie about, his pack and pouches stuffed
With fantasies and condoms; Les King, who crooned
Like Bing, is back from Mareth where he lay,
The tunes mislaid, gargling with his blood.
His songs are out of date. And there are others
Whose faces, though familiar, fade and blur.
The bugle publishes another cry.
Two more commands explode; butts and boots
Crash and ring; another echoing shout
And, by the left, they start to march away.
The steady tramping dims into a mist.
The stone ground stretches in its vacancy;
One final flick of flag, the mist comes down,
And silence stuns with its enormous weight,
And there is nothing left to do but sleep.

Scottsburg USA

'He's a bootlegger,' said the young ladies, moving
somewhere between his cocktails and his flowers.
'One time he killed a man. . . .'

THE GREAT GATSBY

'There was music through the summer nights'.
Zelda was young, an unusual flower,
She swayed in the wind from gold trumpets.
Saxophones sighed for her.

Her sex was a dark nest, warm in the fork
Of white and welcoming branches.
At dawn the barbered lawns
Sparkled with specially imported dew.
The ocean rehearsed its morning performance.
Scott polished the jewel of his gift.
It would last long, longer than he would last.
He would keep it through the slow fall
When the shed leaves deadened the footsteps
Of the pale bailiffs, when the young flower
Grew brittle, crumbling in its expensive vase.
The band packed its instruments and left.
The last guests departed for more hospitable views.
The grass greyed and grew long on the lawns.
Scott walked the streets of winter alone
Where the stores offered only alcohol and accusations.
In sleep his booze-battered, rueful countenance
Looked bitterly wise yet remarkably innocent.
The stone gleamed in a drawer in his desk
Like a small strong lamp in a coffin.
The blinds were drawn.
The long jag was over.

View from a Wheelchair

Every day is visiting day;
There are no temporal restrictions.
You cannot tell them to go away;
They fuss, or are negligent, or bored.
The world is an open ward
Populated by nurses, orderlies,
And simpering visitors with flowers.
I resent with equal rancour
Both indifference and pity.
Children insult me with their agility.
I am an old baby with a blue chin,
At night my teeth snarl in a tumbler.

As evening darkens in my ward
There are voices from beyond,
Clear cries of the unmutilated,
Murmur of sensual conspiracy,
Salutations, prodigal laughter:
The blind effrontery of health.
I will strangle my ears; I will call
And demand to be put to bed.
But I do not pray for a miracle—
You must not deceive yourself there—
And you must not assume my condition
Is not of my own choosing. I am not sure.
I am less unfortunate, maybe,
Than your insolent pity believes:
The muscles in my wheels do not get tired;
Like a horse I can sleep standing.
And there is something sacred about me,
Something that can haunt, and make you tremble.
I am sick of the fear, the pity, the revulsion.
I want them to put me to bed.
Their gratitude for my not being them
Is a nauseous, poisonous toffee.
It is dark and cold. They must put me to bed.
They do not know that I walk in my sleep.

Uncle Edward's Affliction

Uncle Edward was colour-blind;
We grew accustomed to the fact.
When he asked someone to hand him
The green book from the window-seat
And we observed its bright red cover
Either apathy or tact
Stifled comment. We passed it over.
Much later, I began to wonder
What curious world he wandered in,
Down streets where pea-green pillar-boxes

Grinned at a fire-engine as green;
How Uncle Edward's sky at dawn
And sunset flooded marshy green.
Did he ken John Peel with his coat so green
And Robin Hood in Lincoln red?
On country walks avoid being stung
By nettles hot as a witch's tongue?
What meals he savoured with his eyes:
Green strawberries and fresh red peas,
Green beef and greener burgundy.
All unscientific, so it seems:
His world was not at all like that,
So those who claim to know have said.
Yet, I believe, in war-smashed France
He must have crawled from neutral mud
To lie in pastures dark and red
And seen, appalled, on every blade
The rain of innocent green blood.

Any Complaints?

Lawrence—not the bearded one—the one
Who dressed up as a wog and crashed his bike
Doing a ton, if those old jobs could make it then,
Lawrence said something about courage: Courage is like
A bank account; you keep on writing cheques
Until the day comes when there's nothing there,
No more to draw. You're broke. What next?
They tie you to a gunwheel in the lashing air
Or blind you with a bandage and lead you out
As target for small arms.
                          If you are very rich,
Got plenty in that bank, you'll probably get hit
But by the other lot; wind up in a different ditch
But just as dead. With extraordinary luck
You might survive and get back home quite safe.

But what if all your days you've been dead broke,
Never owned a cheque-book in your life,
Nothing in the bank at all?
                              You go to jail
Or try to bluff it out, let others pay your way.
It's not an easy game, and if you fail,
Are shown up as a fraud, no matter what you say
You'll get the gunwheel or the firing-squad.
It isn't fair? All right, but don't tell me.
The Company Commander is the man to see
Or, better still, complain direct to God.

A Kind of Hero

At school he was revered yet lonely.
No other boy, however much
He might dream of it,
Dared to be his friend.
He walked, gaunt and piratical,
All bones and grin,
Towards his inescapable end.

Revered, but not by authority,
He poured ink into the new hat
Of the French Master,
Painted the blackboard white,
Swore at the huge Principal,
Refused to bend
And invited him to a free fight.

In memory he is beautiful,
But only his desperate gold
Hair might have been so.
Vaguely we understood,
And were grateful, that he performed
Our lawless deeds:
Punished, he allowed us to be good.

The end: he was killed at Alamein.
He wore handcuffs on the troopship
Going out: his webbing
All scrubbed as white as rice;
And we, or others like us,
Were promoted
By his last, derisive sacrifice.

View from a Deckchair

I rest in the canvas lap and let fall my book.
The breeze, browsing, flips a few pages,
Leaves it, then comes back for a second look.
My eyelids close, like mouths, on the images.

The sky is green with the smell of crunched grass
Whose dark, shed juice seasons the simmering air;
Eyelids slide open, eyes see a butterfly pass,
Pause, wings frittering, treading the air's water.

Summer mothers me; here I feel secure;
My neighbours are not likely to break down the fences;
The only guns they carry are for making war
On garden pests. Their televisions have valid licences.

Vapour-trails, squeezed out on the bland blue,
Perturb only slightly; the bee's buzz does not sting.
Even when a motorbike rasps in the avenue
The heart bucks only a little, and I stay sitting,

Or, rather, reclining in my garden chair,
And can stay here for at least another hour
Before the benevolent and grass-flavoured air
Loses its warmth, and the chill tastes sour.

Cigarette

It tap-danced on the shining silver case,
Jumped to his mouth, wagged jaunty from teasing lip,
Its whiteness darkening the uncle face;
Thin snake's blue ghost rose curling from the tip.
Emblem of manhood and emancipation,
But something more: it burned yet was renewed
Pure as before; scent stirred sweet perturbation
In the thrilled blood, first inkling of the feud,
Still unresolved, between desire and fear.
My first cigarette was smoked in the boiler shed
Behind the Sunday School in my tenth year.
Veil-dance of smoke revolved in my dazed head,
Strong the sense of falling, though I stood;
I thought that I did wrong, and think so still.
They told us that tobacco-smoking would
Stunt our growth. They tell us now fags kill,
And I believe, though when I ruminate
I see that even smokeless inhalations
Are paces, if not quite so long and straight,
Towards the darkest of all destinations.
I take another, light it, noting how
The stained air holds no sweet reverberations
And that I have no sense of falling now.

View from a Barber's Chair

In the glacial mirror
The skull is preserved;
Dun flesh clings to it
Obstinately alive.
The basin below
Is smooth and white—
Hard flesh of shelled egg—
Taps gleam like spoons.

The head is perched
On a white mound,
Its eyes aggrieved.
Behind, in the gloom,
White deference bends,
Snips and combs;
A glimmer of scissors
Kisses, bites,
Snips locks that, falling,
Tickle the air,
Fall faster than leaves
But quiet and light
On the slope of snow.
Electric buzz
And nibble at neck;
Sweet buzz replies
Warm in the blood;
Surrender's signal,
A yielding hum,
Purred submission
Invite violation,
A numb need
For a cruel Todd,
Which dies away
When the bowing voice
Tickles the ear:
'Next gentleman, please.'
The white mound melts,
Slides down the glass
And disappears.
The stunned head hangs
Amazed a moment,
Then floats away.
The mirror gurgles
In the basin's throat.
The next gentleman
Is gowned in snow.

A Song to Celebrate

Your hair tastes of darkness.
The sea fondles the long drowned.
The shore extends a delicate limb,
The waves relish its whiteness.

Your mouth tastes of moonlight.
The city revs its dark engines;
Lamps are bright burs on the night's coat.
I would wear you like a cloak

And would be your robe for all weathers.
Your flesh tastes of sunlight.
The sea concedes defeat. The drowned
Rise white and dance naked.

Pistol

This one is not black,
Squat, packed with deeper black;
It does not squint.
The silver barrel
Thrusts clean from the chamber
And polished butt's
Mahogany curve
Whose smoothness soothes the hand.
Who would deny
Any healthy boy
Such an old-fashioned and
Beautiful toy?

A Long Sentence

begins slowly, uncertain of
its terminus, but after
the first hesitancies,
destination still hidden,
the pace increases, grows more sure
though with a confidence
that will not be for long sustained
when it becomes apparent
that movement is towards
not revelation or release
but a darkness darker far
than any known midnight,
dungeon, tunnel, desperation,
and all sentences must end
with an abrupt full-stop,
punched in like a nail, its black head
showing on the page, like this.

The Sunday People

After the dolour of bells
The place was shut,
Though at certain intervals
Noises squeezed out
Through venerable walls;
Then all was quiet
Before faint vocables
Told they were out.

The Sunday People, slow
On mournful feet,
A dark irregular queue,
Trickled from the great
Hunk of masonry
And moved through the morning light

As now, through memory,
Linen and faces white.

The smell still lingers; the smell
Of flowers and sick
Comes back when church bells call;
These, too, begin it:
The wax-faced queue who fill
This Sunday memory,
Lovers of hymn and hospital,
Roast beef and cemetery.

Moods of Rain

It can be so tedious, a bore
Telling a long dull story you have heard before
So often it is meaningless;
Yet, in another mood,
It comes swashbuckling, swishing a million foils,
Feinting at daffodils, peppering tin pails,
Pelting so fast on roof, umbrella, hood,
You hear long silk being torn;
Refurbishes old toys, and oils
Slick surfaces that gleam as if unworn.
Sometimes a cordial summer rain will fall
And string on railings delicate small bells;
Soundless as seeds on soil
Make green ghosts rise.
It can be fierce, hissing like blazing thorns,
Or side-drums hammering at night-filled eyes
Until you wake and hear a long grief boil
And, overflowing, sluice
The lost raft of the world.
Yet it can come as lenitive and calm
As comfort from the mother of us all
Sighing you into sleep
Where peace prevails and only soft rains fall.

Mercenaries

At first we were attracted by the pure
Thrill of playing childish games with all
The seriousness of children; or, unsure
Of our own strength, our stamina and will,
Enlisted, hoping to survive the test;
Others liked the reckless uniform.
But one lure winked that no one could resist,
The dream that strengthened all and kept us warm
On cold patrols and lonely nights on guard,
A fantasy of total anarchy
Made flesh at last, the marvellous reward
Of absolute permission, liberty
That babies, lunatics and millionaires,
And they alone, are able to afford:
The spoils of war, the naked town sprawled out
Inviting us to enter and enjoy.
But when—the last defenders put to rout—
We seized the city like a promised toy,
The most inviting doors were booby-trapped,
The wine was sour, they'd buried all the gold;
The dogs and children snarled and cursed and snapped,
And every woman was gun-hard and cold.

Black Dog

Across grass gnawed by dingy snow
Half-thawed, now frozen, a soiled shroud
Patched and torn on a cold torso,
The dog prowls on numb pads;
The dark hedge drinks his darker shape
And he is gone.
                        The last light rots,
Crumbles to night; the cold clamps hard.
Grey rats freeze on the ditch's verge;

The lane is smeared with gritty lard.
Time to go home. Yet no desire.
The black dog waits, sprawled by the fire;
In that small house looks very large,
Owns all within, including those
Soft furnishings that ache and age.

Dreamgirl

Her name is not important. On the screen
Or front page of the polished magazine
What slaps you in the eyballs is her tits,
Soft bombs whose threats to burst score accurate hits;
The mouth your eyes can taste, her ripened eyes
Before which all equivocation dies;
Lithe legs and gorgeous haunches spread and curve
On red divan of tight sprung vein and nerve.

You want her. Yes. But reason intervenes:
She cannot really be just what she seems.
If fantasy should muscle into fact,
Surely you'd find her actual presence lacked
The opulence her image offered you:
If not a lie, then not entirely true;
Some artifice, small sympathy; worse still,
Cold waxwork lacking passion, needs or skill.

But Brother, eye to keyhole, have you thought?
Behind the door might lie a different sort
Of creature, someone much more terrible,
Whose writhings, far from being artificial,
Would flush with blood, would sweat and burn and grip,
Whose five-thonged need would flog you like a whip.
Stay kneeling there; reality can bite.
Settle for screen and page. You've got good eyesight.

No Sense of Direction

I have always admired
Those who are sure
Which turning to take,
Who need no guide
Even in war
When thunders shake
The torn terrain,
When battalions of shrill
Stars all desert
And the derelict moon
Goes over the hill:
Eyes chained by the night
They find their way back
As if it were daylight.
Then, on peaceful walks
Over strange wooded ground,
They will find the right track,
Know which of the forks
Will lead to the inn
I would never have found;
For I lack their gift,
Possess almost no
Sense of direction.
And yet I owe
A debt to this lack,
A debt so vast
No reparation
Can ever be made,
For it led me away
From the road I sought
Which would carry me to—
I mistakenly thought—
My true destination:
It made me stray
To this lucky path
That ran like a fuse
And brought me to you

And love's bright, soundless
Detonation.

Summer in the Park

Sun leans lightly on all temples;
In the park the far trees
Melt at their shadowed knees.
Summer supplies its simples
For all but one disease:
Young dogs, young sons, young mothers,
Gold waterfall hair of daughters
Float over trim green seas.
He could munch them up and swallow them,
Yes, even the melting trees,
The staid man on the seat
Whose heart's teeth ache with love
And its impossible sweet.

Blood Letter

Frail leech that craves an open vein,
Paper vampire, blood-letter,
Go in your mild envelope
Disguised as harmless paper.

Dissemble in the postman's sack,
Mix with football coupons, views
Of beaches, blackmail, racing tips,
Poems and domestic news.

Go to her whose heart your need is,
But temper your red hunger, rest
Gently on her pulses, be
Tender at her breast.

And hope that she will welcome you
To ease her fever and make better
Such distemper as she suffers,
Letter of blood, love-letter.

Growing Pain

The boy was barely five years old.
We sent him to the little school
And left him there to learn the names
Of flowers in jam jars on the sill
And learn to do as he was told.
He seemed quite happy there until
Three weeks afterwards, at night,
The darkness whimpered in his room.
I went upstairs, switched on his light,
And found him wide awake, distraught,
Sheets mangled and his eiderdown
Untidy carpet on the floor.
I said, 'Why can't you sleep? A pain?'
He snuffled, gave a little moan,
And then he spoke a single word:
'Jessica.' The sound was blurred.
'Jessica? What do you mean?'
'A girl at school called Jessica,
She hurts—' he touched himself between
The heart and stomach '—she has been
Aching here and I can see her.'
Nothing I had read or heard
Instructed me in what to do.
I covered him and stroked his head.
'The pain will go, in time,' I said.

The Toys of Love

His cuddly toy of love
Was bought to keep him warm;
In bed he held it tight
And did not fear the storm
Which flogged the howling night
Until it bled to dawn.

His woolly toy of love
No longer soft and white
Grew bristly, cold and thin,
Consoled no more at night;
Its mouth chewed on a grin,
Showed teeth and they could bite.

His silver gift of love
He used with joy and skill
And wore it on his thigh,
Was thrilled by it until
He found it was no toy,
Was loaded, and could kill.

A Quaint Disorder

A quaint disorder, this:
I do not sleep too well
For fear the dark hours build
A solitary cell;
My intellect expels
Its former policies,
Disburdened can explore
Remoter galaxies.
My heart snarls at the way
The minutes pitter past

Towards the last abyss.
I tremble at the vast
Arsenals that Chance
Commands, could call upon
To lay mines in your path.
The moonlight that once shone
Benignly frightens me,
As does deceitful air;
Time's frequent felonies
Are crueller than they were.
Food no longer tempts
The withered appetite;
I hunger only for
That longed-for, good tonight
When you, desired physician,
Will come with healing art
And magical prescription
To purge my febrile heart
Of all its grave distempers
And burn my fever-chart.
A quaint disorder, this,
Which stabs with hope and doubt,
And one—with all its pains—
I would not be without.

A Game of Shove-Ha'penny

.

In a pub in Hampstead on a Spring evening
A couple were playing shove-ha'penny. They wore
The uniform of the district and of youth:
Sweater, jeans and unwrinkled skin.
Her bottom and breasts were roundly confident
And her hair was dark with a gleam of copper
Within. The man was dark and thin.

He bent over the table playing that game
With bitter concentration. She took her turn

But her play was more perfunctory. She wept.
She shoved the discs across the board
And, all the time, the tears blurted from her eyes
And moved down her face like little snails; they left
A pale brown spoor where they had crept.

For a long time they did not speak. Then he turned,
Looked at her directly; his eyes jabbed hate.
He cursed her, but she did not respond except
To deliver another tear.
His stare was without pity, informing her
That pain is not like beauty: only its host
Is moved by it when love is not there.

The Rivals

All, all of them wanted her.
I watched them, ready to frustrate
Whatever strategy they used,
Doubly armed with fear and hate:
Prince Mincing and Lord Bulge were there,
Paul Profile and Lance Glitterteeth,
Sir Timothy Tarmac, hand on hilt
And golden blade half out of sheath.
I blocked her view when they came flaunting
Their wealth, fine clothes, virility,
Firm jaw, white smile of dancing master;
I showed my own agility.
But there was one whose gaunt appeal
I had not reckoned with. She fell
For him, the one I'd overlooked,
She, with her dainty sense of smell,
Fastidious ways, she fell for him,
The bony one with stinking breath
And sergeant's stripes, the clever fellow
In whose small room she lies beneath
A stiff cold quilt, without a pillow.

The Moth

'The moth has got into it.'
I heard the woman speak from another room.
What the moth had entered I did not know,
Nor why that singular creature should own
The definite article before its name.
The woman said 'The moth' as she might say
'The dog', a minor member of the family,
Yet in my mind's commodious bestiary
There was no space for such a stray.
I knew that it was time for me to go.
I crept away. I left some clothes:
A sweater, vest, two pairs of socks with holes.
Sometimes I think of the moth in its cage,
Its great khaki wings heavy with dust
And the woman feeding it, pushing through the bars
The tasteless garments to assuage
An appetite that must
Make do with such rough food as she, too, must.

Wife Killer

He killed his wife at night.
He had tried once or twice in the daylight
But she refused to die.

In darkness the deed was done,
Not crudely with a hammer-hard gun
Or strangler's black kid gloves on.

She just ceased being alive,
Not there to interfere or connive,
Linger, leave or arrive.

It seemed almost as though
Her death was quite normal and no
Clue to his part would show.

So then, with impunity,
He called up that buttocky beauty
He had so long longed to see

All covering gone: the double
Joggle of warm weighty bubbles
Was sweet delirious trouble.

And all night, all night he enjoyed her;
Such sport in her smooth dimpled water;
Then daylight came like a warder.

And he rose and went down to the larder
Where the mouse-trap again had caught a
Piece of stale gorgonzola.

His wife wore her large woollen feet.
She said that he was late
And asked what he wanted to eat,

But said nothing about the murder—
And who, after all, could have told her?
He said that he fancied a kipper.

Death in the Lounge Bar

The bar he went inside was not
A place he often visited;
He welcomed anonymity;
No one to switch inquisitive
Receivers on, no one could see,
Or wanted to, exactly what

He was, or had been, or would be;
A quiet brown place, a place to drink
And let thought simmer like good stock,
No mirrors to distract, no fat
And calculating face of clock,
A good calm place to sip and think.
If anybody noticed that
He was even there they'd see
A fairly tall and slender man,
Fair-haired, blue-eyed, and handsome in
A manner strictly masculine.
They would not know, or want to know,
More than what they saw of him,
Nor would they wish to bug the bone
Walls of skull and listen in
To whatever whisperings
Pittered quietly in that dark:
An excellent place to sip your gin.
Then—sting of interruption! voice
Pierced the private walls and shook
His thoughtful calm with delicate shock.
A waiter, with white napkin face
And shining toe-cap hair, excused
The oiled intrusion, asking if
His name was what indeed it was.
In that case he was wanted on
The telephone the customers used,
The one next to the Gents. He went.
Inside the secretive warm box
He heard his wife's voice, strangled by
Distance, darkness, coils of wire,
But unmistakably her voice,
Asking why he was so late,
Why did he humiliate
Her in every way he could,
Make her life so hard to face?
She'd telephoned most bars in town
Before she'd finally tracked him down.
He said that he'd been working late
And slipped in for a quick one on

His weary journey home. He'd come
Back at once. Right now. Toot sweet.
No, not another drop. Not one.
Back in the bar, he drank his gin
And ordered just one more, the last.
And just as well: his peace had gone;
The place no longer welcomed him.
He saw the waiter moving past,
That pale ambassador of gloom,
And called him over, asked him how
He had known which customer
To summon to the telephone.
The waiter said, 'Your wife described
You, sir. I knew you instantly.'
'And how did she describe me, then,
That I'm so easily recognized?'
'She said: grey suit, cream shirt, blue tie,
That you were fairly tall, red-faced,
Stout, middle-aged, and going bald.'
Disbelief cried once and sat
Bolt upright, then it fell back dead.
'Stout middle-aged and going bald.'
The slender ghost with golden hair
Watched him go into the cold
Dark outside, heard his slow tread
Fade towards wife, armchair, and bed.

A Simple Need

Well, no. Not now I suppose. Not now.
Not in the eyes of the law, I'm not any longer
Married. Yet still I feel she belongs to me,
In a way. Not that she ever really did,
Belong to me I mean. Right from the start I felt
That she was marking time, rehearsing, using me
As stand-in for the genuine first night.
Well, time will mark her in its own good time,

Though that's not what I want. I'm not vindictive.
I'd hate to see her sucked dry by the years.
She always seemed so ripe. I used to think
She's like a plum, a big plum with the smooth
Bloom on summer skin, a plum of plums,
The way they halve! Ridiculous, I know.
But listen, let me tell you something. Listen.
I never caught her out. I never once.
I'd come back two days early from a trip,
Wait till the lights were out. I'd leave the car
A block away and creep up pussyfoot.
I never caught them at it. Never once.
The joke is she got rid of me. Cruelty she said.
I can't go near. Not now. They'd jail me if I did.
But one of these fine nights I'll go,
I've got to go. Just to see them at it once,
That's all. Just see the two of them.
It's only fair.
Drink up. We've time for just one more.
That's all I want: Just see them at it once.

The Mourners

The boy was dead, his body lay
In the smart box.
The vicar said that death and life
Compose a paradox.

Maybe. I watched the father, who
Had not seen
His son for eighteen months or more,
Face raised like a tragic queen;

Tears candidly confessed his grief,
Marched from his eyelids,
Medalled his cheeks. Some time now since
He left his wife and kids.

No histrionics from the wife,
No jewellery of tears;
She would leave for home, a cold house,
Light lamps against her fears,

Build fires against the evening chill,
And yet not cry;
Feed the living children; pray
That none of these would die.

Fear of the Dark

Along the unlit lane on a night
When the stars are blind, the moon masked,
Footsteps follow. I knew a man
Of six foot three who, on dark nights,
Held two lit cigarettes between his lips
Hoping by this bright stratagem
To fox footpads, mislead murderers.
I used to laugh at him, but not now.
I clench teeth and fists and walk fast.
When I reach the house I switch on lights.
The darkness seems defeated, yet
Open the door, the light does not flow far
Beyond the threshold; it stops dead
A few feet from the step, I hear
The darkness growing; it is enormous,
It is in this room in thin disguise.
I am afraid of it, and with good reason.

THE WINTER MAN
1973

Comeback

The wind is in a whipping mood tonight.
Whatever changes, these old noises don't.
My Grandad must have heard it much the same
And lain in bed and known that sleep had gone
To find a quieter place.

                              When I was twelve,
And that's a good half century ago,
I used to lie awake, not that the wind
Could scare sleep from my bed, but something could:
A sharp electric charge of restlessness
Would needle and excite for hours on end,
And, in imagination, I would touch
Each object of my shadow treasury—
An odd collection for a kid to love—
Not foreign stamps or hollow eggs in beds
Of cotton-wool, not model aeroplanes
Or rolling-stock, nor hoarded coins or cards,
But articles of apparatus, kit
And clothing of a special usefulness,
The paraphernalia of the fighter's craft.
It seems unlikely now that all that gear,
Which came to be the tackle and the tools
Of my life's trade, could thrill me in those days
As later only women's secrets could.
Yet that's the way it was, and even now
I catch a tiny tremor of the old
Excitement on the sagging wires of nerve
Recalling how I'd lay the objects out—
The black kid boots, white ankle-socks, the gloves
Like giant kidneys, skipping-rope and towel,
The glittering robe embroidered on the back
With my brave name; black satin trunks
With yellow stripes and wide band at the waist;
And no less sacred, no less magical,
The grim and necessary armour of
Gum-shield, jockstrap and protective cup.

Not that I really owned these things. Not then.
The only kit I had for training nights
Was my old sand-shoes, cotton football shorts
And winter vest. But one day I would wear
The finest stuff. I knew I'd make the big time,
And I did.

>   *Listen to that wind.*
> *It's strange how all its anger comforts you,*
> *Maybe because it means I'm not alone;*
> *We share the long hours of the night, the two*
> *Of us, the old and tireless wind and me.*
> *Does the wind have memories to shuffle through?*
> *If so, they can't be very cheerful ones,*
> *Judging by that sound.*

                    Oh, yes, I knew
I'd get to be a champion one day,
Though that was not the most important thing.
Important, yes, but what meant more to me
Was making myself good enough to wear
The garb the great ones wore. And even more
Important was the pleasure in the game,
Though 'pleasure' seems too weak a word for that
Drench of power that filled you when you fought
And overcame with cunning, speed and skill
A tough opponent. Many times I've made
A perfect move, smooth as satin, quick as a cat,
The muscles thinking faster than a wink,
A double feint and counter, something you
Could never in a thousand lessons teach
An ordinary fighter to perform:
A miracle, a gift. Those moments make
Your life worthwhile.

                    The other stuff was muck:
I mean the silver trophies, medals, praise;
And later, fighting pro, the fancy belts,
The pictures on the sports page, interviews,

The youngsters scrambling for your scribbled name,
Even the big-time purses and the girls,
The bitches who would suck the virtue from you,
Press near your fame until the glitter dimmed,
They'd smear you with their artificial honey
And leave you spoiled and shamed.

                    I think it's strange
That when you've reached the top and won the crown
And every childish fantasy is fact,
It's strange how disappointing it all seems.
Success and fame, I've had the two and found
That both were fragile as those eggshell globes
They hang on Christmas trees. I used to think
The boys who'd never made the top, the ones
Who fought for peanuts in the shabby halls
And lost more often than they won, I thought
Them pitiable. Not now. They never knew
The failure of success, and they were real
Members of our craft, good workmen, proud
To wear the badges of the trade, a breed
That, if it dies, would surely mean the end
Of what I still believe the greatest game.

                    I won my first
Big title at the Albert Hall.
I fought a good old-timer from the North,
Birkenhead I think it was. He knew
The moves, was cagey as a monkey-house,
But he was past his best and in the seventh
I felt him weaken; as his strength seeped out
I seemed to suck it in like Dracula.
I put him down three times and in the ninth
He took a fast right-cross and folded up.
I knew he wouldn't rise. I did my dance
Above his fallen body, and the crowd
Bellowed their brainless worship of my feat.
I never thought that night my turn would come,
That eight years later in the selfsame ring
My nose would squash against the dust and resin

As I lay flat; I'd hear the same applause
But for the other man, new champion,
A youngster, strong, ambitious, arrogant.
By that time I had fought in Canada,
Twice at the Garden in New York, Berlin,
Milan and Paris, Rome, the Blackfriars Ring
And Stadium Club and places I've forgot.
I'd made and spent a fortune for those days,
And now they wrote me off. Another fool
Who once had been a fighter, now a ghost,
A fading name in yellowing papers, soon
Remembered only by a very few
And even they would get the details wrong
And, after too much booze, remember fights
I'd never had.

         The wind is dying down
But still it makes its music, now less wild
But melancholy. It seems to sense my mood.
I doubt if I shall sleep tonight at all.
To tell the truth I have a taste for that
Sad sound of wind with darkness in its throat;
I like it when it snatches rain like seeds,
Throws handfuls at the window. But tonight
Is dry. No rain. No sleep. Only the wind
And memories.

         After that defeat
I drank too much. I played the horses, too,
And lost the little capital I'd saved.
I was not old—a little over thirty—
Young enough in years, but I had fought
Two hundred contests as a pro, was tired.
But there was nothing else to do but fight.
It was my trade, the only one I knew.
And so I made my comeback, cut out booze,
Began to train with rope and heavy bag,
Run in the misty mornings through the park
And spar in the gym at night. I got a fight

In Leeds and put my man away in three.
I went back to the Club and showed them there
I still knew more about my business than
Those youngsters with their blasting energy
But little sense of what to do with it:
They sprayed their shots all round the field of fire;
I hoarded ammunition, only pressed
The trigger when I knew my shots would tell.
Once more my name appeared in fresh black ink,
My picture on a million breakfast tables.
They matched me for the title once again.
The fight was held in summer, out of doors,
White City was the place. The night was fine
And thousands came to see the veteran
Hand out a lesson to the cheeky boy
Who called himself the Champion. I knew
I'd win the title back. I'd seen him fight:
He was young and strong, with fair ability,
But I was master of a hundred tricks
He'd never heard about. I might be old
But I was also wise.

                         The fight began
At nine o'clock at night as dark came down.
The arc-lamps gushed white brilliance on the ring.
Beyond the ropes, the crowd, a factory
Of noise and appetites, was idling now
Though very soon I knew the huge machine
Would roar to tumult, hammer out acclaim,
And I would be the target of that praise.
The comeback would succeed, though history
Was littered with the names of those who'd failed.
I would not fail.

                         The first round proved to me
That my opponent was no better than
A score of fighters I had met before
And beaten easily. I jabbed and moved,
Slipping his leads and hurting him inside.
I took my time, collected points and foiled

His two attempts to trap me on the ropes.
The round was mine.

                              The second round began
With brisker action from us both; he swung
A left and followed with an uppercut
Slung hard towards my heart. I moved away,
Stepped in and jabbed and jolted back his head;
I saw my chance and threw a big right hand.
I felt the jar to elbow as my fist
Connected with his jaw. He should have gone.
Most would. He staggered back but did not fall.
The engines of applause were roaring wild.
He faded back. I knew I had him then.
I took my time. I was too old a hand
To crowd in, throwing leather at his head.
I stalked him to the ropes and measured him:
A feint downstairs, a jab—I saw his chin
And threw again the punch to douse the lights—
I never knew what happened. Something burst
Inside my head; my skull was opened up
And starless midnight flooded into it.
I'll never know what happened on that night,
Why my right fist did not connect and end
The fight with me as Champion. They said
He beat me to the punch. Maybe. It seemed
A thunderbolt had fallen from the skies,
A biblical defeat, the fall of Pride.
One thing was sure: I had not won the bout
Nor would I ever have another chance.
I'd never be a champion again.

                              I said that I'd retire,
Hang up the gloves for good, but very soon
I went into the ring, though now I knew
That I would never make the top again.
I fought in little halls and local baths,
Making a pound or two but taking some
Beatings from boys who five years earlier

Could not have laced my shoes. Sometimes I'd dream
That I would even yet surprise them all,
Come back and dazzle them with my old skill.
I nursed the dream till not so long ago
And then I gave myself a shake and said,
'Stop acting like a kid. You're grown up now.'
I got a job as trainer at a club
In Bermondsey. It's fine. I like it there.
I taught those boys some things they'd never learn
From amateurs. I still work there. It's good.
I like to see them in the ring. I like
The smell of rubbing oils, to hear the swish
And slap of skipping-rope, the thud of fist
On bag. I like it all. I don't complain.
I'm quite a lucky man.

                       The windows pale.
The wind itself seems tired now. I lie
Stretched out, but not to take the final count;
I have a round or two left in me yet.
My body is my own biography:
The scars, old fractures, ribs and nose, thick ear;
That's what I am, a score of ancient wounds
And in my head a few remembered scenes
And even those I'm not too sure about—
I've heard them say my brains are scrambled now—
I'm not too sure. Not sure of anything,
Except I'm proud of what I've been—although
I would have liked another chance—sure, too,
I'll never make another comeback now
Unless the dead can make it, as some say.

Here and Human

In the warm room, cushioned by comfort,
Idle at fireside, shawled in lamplight,
I know the cold winter night, but only

As a far intimation, like a memory
Of a dead distress whose ghost has grown genial.

The disc, glossy black as a conjuror's hat,
Revolves. Music is unwound: woodwind,
Strings, a tenor voice singing in a tongue
I do not comprehend or have need to—
'The instrument of egoism mastered by art'—

For what I listen to is unequivocal:
A distillation of romantic love,
Passion outsoaring speech. I understand
And, understanding, I rejoice in my condition:
This sweet accident of being here and human.

Later, as I lie in the dark, the echoes
Recede, the blind cat of sleep purrs close
But does not curl. Beyond the window
The hill is hunched under his grey cape
Like a watchman. I cannot hear his breathing.

Silence is a starless sky on the ceiling
Till shock slashes, stillness is gashed
By a dazzle of noise chilling the air
Like lightning. It is an animal screech,
Raucous, clawing: surely the language of terror.

But I misread it, deceived. It is the sound
Of passionate love, a vixen's mating call.
It lingers hurtful, a stink in the ear,
But soon it begins to fade. I breathe deep,
Feeling the startled fur settle and smooth. Then I sleep.

The Discriminator

I can afford to discriminate
In the matter of female pulchritude,

Though I will readily admit
That, to many observers, my attitude
Must seem pernickety, even absurd.
This, of course, is not the way of it
Though I understand why the less fastidious
Call me poseur or hypocrite.
Take that girl over there—fine tits
I will concede, but her ankles are too thick.
Her eyes are pleasing, opalescent, dark
As a glass of stout held up to light,
But the mouth is so slack as to make you sick.
Her blonde companion, I must remark,
Is far too wide in the hips. She might
Be pretty enough, but in a style
So commonplace you must have seen
The same face in a hundred city streets.
I note your disbelieving smile.
Don't be deceived, young man; the time
Will come when you, too, will apply
The cool astringent judgement you observe
Me exercising now. Your eye
Will be, as mine, fastidious and cold,
And you will then display the fine
Wisdom and discernment of the old,
Enjoy the wages of experience,
Reject expediency and compromise
With the stern impartiality of age
And age's impotence.

The Defrauded Woman Speaks

The legend of my love and its defeat
Is soiled and crushed beneath indifferent feet.
Excrement and mud are smeared across
The words that cannot apprehend my loss.
I'm reckoned as pathetic or a joke,
Perhaps a bit of both. They say: 'She's broke.

He's robbed her of her savings, every cent,
A cool twelve thousand, all the lot he spent
On other, younger women.' And it's true.
I'm broke all right, and broken-hearted, too,
Though not because of all I had to spend
But just because the whole thing had to end.
I was not fooled, was always well aware
That he was lying, but I did not care.
The other women hurt, but what hurts more
Is that I'd never known such joy before
And never will again. You wonder why
I went into the box to testify
Against him. Vengeance maybe. I don't know.
One thing I'm absolutely sure of, though,
And this is it: I swear I'd gladly give
However many years I've left to live
For just another month with him; again
To hear his sweet deceitful whisper feign
A lovelier love than plain and honest fare;
To feel his hands exploring flesh and hair,
Re-educating lust until it knew
How false such categories as false and true.

Confrontation

When we finally met, the hatred
That for weeks had been savoured
Was drained of taste;
We let it fall.
We looked at each other without fear,
With shyness and curiosity,
No loathing at all.

The impulse to smash bone and tear flesh
Was gone; no aftertaste
Lingered and sickened.
One did not forgive.

Forgiveness and blame were irrelevant
As knuckle-duster, cosh, revolver,
Or slick shiv.

My need was for the affection
I felt for him, and he
I am sure wanted mine.
Courteously we waited,
Uncertain, yet each with the knowledge
That through the bonds of her body
We were related.

I felt a rare generosity,
A kinship and sympathy;
Believed, in us both,
These might uncover
New areas of magnanimity,
Dismissing such trivia as who
Was husband and who lover.

Love Nest

Perched high, it swayed when the wind was wild.
Roots were loosening in the stone.
It was not safe. Underground thunder
Rumbled, made it jerk and shudder.
He knew one day, or rather night,
The nest must fall: the place of loving
Was the place of death. He saw the picture:
Their fallen bodies on the ground,
Soldered together like a single creature,
Without a stitch or feather on,
For the world and his wife to look upon.

Picture of the Bride

Alone, among the grey crosses and stones,
The slabs of marble, slippery as brawn,
Absolute as theirs the stillness she owns;
Her whiteness darkens the shades on the lawn.

Her features are hidden under the veil
Which also conceals the gleam of her hair;
Sepulchral she seems, not humanly frail,
Whiter and taller than any tomb there.

Sleeping Beauty

It was evening when he reached the place.
Outside, the air was motionless.
He listened for the sound of sigh or snore.
Silence trickled down his face;
He touched his sword for confidence,
Then parted the dark foliage at the door.

He entered. She was beautiful.
He pressed his mouth to hers; her lips
Grew warm and parted, breathing quick yet deep;
Her waking welcome magical,
Until her sharp teeth came to grips
And munched; for she was starved from that long sleep.

A Mystery at Euston

The train is still, releasing one loud sigh.
Doors swing and slam, porters importune.

The pigskin labelled luggage of the rich
Is piled on trolleys, rolled to waiting cars,
Grey citizens lug baggage to the place
Where fluttering kisses, craning welcomes wait.
A hoarse voice speaks from heaven, but not to her,
The girl whose luggage is a tartan grip
With broken zip, white face a tiny kite
Carried on the currents of the crowd.
The handsome stranger did not take her bag,
No talent-scout will ask her out to dine.
Her tights are laddered and her new shoes wince.
The Wimpy bar awaits, the single room,
The job as waitress, golden-knuckled ponce.
Whatever place she left—Glasgow, Leeds,
The village on the moors—there's no return.
Beyond the shelter of the station, rain
Veils the day and wavers at a gust,
Then settles to its absent-minded work
As if it has forgotten how to rest.

The Widow's Complaint

You left as you so often left before,
Sneaking out on tiptoe,
No slam of door,
Off to drink with enemies of mine,
And of yours—
If you could only see it—
Drunkards and bores
Whose grossest flatteries
You swilled down with the booze
That you never had the gumption to refuse.
You won't come back this time.
No need to prepare
A welcome for you—clamped silence
And belligerent stare—

No need for morning nostrums or to hide
The whisky and car-keys,
Tighten my lips and thighs
Against your pleas,
No need for those old stratagems any more.
But you might have let me know what was in store;
Your last low trick
To leave me with no clue
That you had gone for good,
My last chance lost
To tell you what I've so long wanted to,
How much I hate you and I always have,
You pig, you bastard,
Stinking rat—
Oh, love, my love,
How can I forgive you that?

Five Domestic Interiors

I

The lady of the house is on her benders;
She's scrubbed and mopped until her knees are sore.
She rests a second as her husband enters,
Then says, 'Look out! Don't walk on my clean floor.'
He looks up at the slick flies on the ceiling
And shakes his head, and goes back through the door.

II

She holds her chuckling baby to her bosom
And says, 'My honey-pie, my sugar bun,
Does Mummy love her scrumptious little darling?
You're lovely, yes, you are, my precious one!'
But when the little perisher starts bawling
She says, 'For God's sake listen to your son.'

III

Sandbagged by sleep at last the kids lie still.
The kitchen clock is nodding in warm air.
They spread the Sunday paper on the table
And each draws up a comfortable chair.
He turns the pages to the crossword puzzle,
Nonplussed they see a single large black square.

IV

The radio is playing dated music
With lilac tune and metronomic beat.
She smiles and says, 'Remember that one, darling?
The way we used to foxtrot was a treat.'
But they resist the momentary temptation
To resurrect slim dancers on glib feet.

V

In bed his tall enthusiastic member
Receives warm welcome, and a moist one too.
She whispers, 'Do you love me? More than ever?'
And, panting, he replies, 'Of course I do.'
Then as she sighs and settles close for slumber
He thinks, with mild surprise, that it is true.

Song for a Winter Birth

Under the watchful lights
    A child was born;
From a mortal house of flesh
    Painfully torn.

And we, who later assembled
    To praise or peer,
Saw merely an infant boy
    Sleeping there.

Then he awoke and stretched
  Small arms wide
And for food or comfort
  Quavering cried.

A cry and attitude
  Rehearsing in small
The deathless death still haunting
  The Place of the Skull.

Outside, in the festive air,
  We lit cigars.
The night was nailed to the sky
  With hard bright stars.

Cold Spell

Take a black length of water,
                leave it rippling as the day dies,
By morning it will be stretched taut,
                pale and motionless, stiff silk.
Take a solitary puddle,
                let it be nursed under sharp stars,
At dawn it will be a small blind mirror,
                cold and milky.
The field in a single night
                will age, grizzle and grow brittle;
Grasses will welcome destruction,
                crunching underfoot.
Take a deep inhalation
                and release slowly,
In the scentless air you will see
                drifting bundles of breath.
Take a look at the sycamore and oak trees,
                they will shame your softness
With their black calisthenics
                gaunt against grey sky.

At sunset the dark cottage windows
                    will flush with a vinous infusion.
The furrows of mud in the field
                    might break a careless toe.
The cold spell works. Listen:
                    you can hear
The tap of hammers, the scrape of chisel,
                    the silver engines.
For disenchantment you must draw
                    fur and fire
Close, close to you, or better,
                    embrace a live body,
Drink broth of warm breath,
                    eat each other.

Picnic on the Lawn

Their dresses were splashed on the green
Like big petals; polished spoons shone
And tinkered with cup and saucer.
Three women sat there together.

They were young, but no longer girls.
Above them the soft green applause
Of leaves acknowledged their laughter.
Their voices moved at a saunter.

Small children were playing nearby;
A swing hung from an apple tree
And there was a sand pit for digging.
Two of the picnicking women

Were mothers. The third was not.
She had once had a husband, but
He had gone to play the lover
With a new lead in a different theatre.

157

One of the mothers said, 'Have you
Cherished a dream, a fantasy
You know is impossible; a childish
Longing to do something wildly

'Out of character? I'll tell you mine.
I would like to drive alone
In a powerful sports car, wearing
A headscarf and dark glasses, looking

'Sexy and mysterious and rich.'
The second mother smiled: 'I wish
I could ride through an autumn morning
On a chestnut mare, cool wind blowing

'The jet black hair I never had
Like smoke streaming from my head.
In summer, swoop on a switchback sea
Surf-riding in a black bikini.'

She then turned to the childless one:
'And you? You're free to make dreams true.
You have no need of fantasies
Like us domestic prisoners.'

A pause, and then the answer came:
'I also have a hopeless dream:
Tea on the lawn in a sunny garden,
Listening to the voices of my children.'

End of a Season

The nights are drawing in; the daylight dies
With more dispatch each evening;
Traffic draws lit beads
Across the bridge's abacus.

Below, black waters jitter in a breeze.
The air is not yet cold
But woven in its woof of various blues,
Whiffs of petrol and cremated flowers,
A cunning thread runs through,
A thin premonitory chill.
The parks are closed. Lights beckon from the bars.
The sporting news has put on heavier dress.
It is not autumn yet
Though summer will not fill
Attentive hearts again with its warm yes.

Far from the city, too, the dark surprises:
Oak and sycamore hunch
Under their loads of leaves;
Plump apples fall; the night devises
Frail webs to vein the sleek skin of the plums.
The scent of stars is cold.
The wheel-ruts stumble in the lane, are dry and hard.
Night is a nest for the unhatched cries of owls;
As deep mines clench their gold
Night locks up autumn's voices in
The vaults of silence. Hedges are still shawled
With traveller's joy; yet windows of the inn
Rehearse a winter welcome.
Though tomorrow may be fine
Soon it will yield to night's swift drawing in.

The athletes of light evenings hibernate;
Their whites are folded round
Green stains; the night
Reminds with its old merchandise—
Those summer remnants on its highest boughs—
That our late dancing days
Are doomed if not already under ground.
The playground gates are chained; the swings hang still;
The lovers have come down
From their deciduous hill;
Others may climb again, but they will not.

And yet the heart resumes its weightier burden
With small reluctance; fares
Towards Fall, and then beyond
To winter with whom none can fool or bargain.

Beside the Sea

Dark as braves, red as bricks from kilns
Or brown as loaves from ovens,
The faces of the veterans confirm
That the business of the sun had flourished
Before this diligent rain began.

And sun will hammer out its gold again,
Though when it does the gloom
Inside the heart and head will not disperse
Entirely: beneath the shimmering
Exuberance dark threads will creep,

Will drag against the flow, cold undertow,
While various boats put out
For trips across the bay, and on the beach
Little fists are fastened round
Olympic cones of frozen fire.

Sand will be slapped and deck-chairs fatten, groan,
As naked boys conceal
Their willies under prudently hung towels
And shops will flush with smooth pink rock
Seductive under cellophane.

But, as the sun presides and we applaud,
Dejection will persist,
A mist from off the sea, invisible,
Whose clinging weight will lie upon
The spirits like damp clouts.

Deny it as we might while daylight cries
With gulls and objurgations,
With noon's delight and shine,
At night we know, hearing its far, caged roar,
The greed and true vocation of the sea.

Incident at West Bay

He drove on to the quay.
His children, Mark and Jane,
Shrilled their needs:
A ride in a boat for Mark,
Ice-cream and the sands for Jane.

Gulls banked and glided over
The nudging dinghies; waves
Mildly admonished
The walls with small slaps.
It was the first day of the holidays.

'Wait there,' he said, 'I'll bring
Ice-cream.' Out of the car
He felt the breeze
Easing the vehemence of the sun.
He said, 'I won't be long.'

He walked a few steps before
He was hit by a shout; he spun
Quickly round
To see his car begin
To move to the edge of the quay.

It was blind; it could not see.
It did not hesitate
But toppled in.
The sea was shocked, threw up
Astonished lace-cuffed waves.

He ran, he followed, plunged,
And in the shifting green gloom
He saw the car's
Tipped shape; he clutched handle, lugged.
His lungs bulged, punishing.

Through glass he saw their faces
Float, eyes wide as hunger,
Staring mouths,
Their lost and sightless hands.
In his chest the sea heaved

And pressed, swelled black and burst
Flooding his skull; it dragged
Him up to air.
They hauled him out and spread him
Oozing on the slimed stone.

They pumped the salt and darkness
From his lungs and skull;
Light scoured his eyes.
The sun said, 'Rise.' The gulls
Fell silent, then echoed his long torn yell.

Battlefields

Tonight in the pub I talked with Ernie Jones
Who served with the Somersets in Normandy,
And we remembered how our fathers told
The sad and muddy legends of their war,
And how, as youngsters, we would grin and say:
'The old man's on his favourite topic now,
He never tires of telling us the tale.'
We are the old men now, our turn has come.
The names have changed—Tobruk and Alamein,
Arnhem, the Falaise Gap and Caen Canal

Displace the Dardanelles, Gallipoli,
Vimy Ridge, the Somme—but little else.
Our children do not want to hear about
The days when we were young and, sometimes, brave,
And who can blame them? Certainly not us.
We drank a last half pint and said goodnight.
And now, at home, the family is in bed,
The kitchen table littered with crashed planes;
A tank is tilted on its side, one track
Has been blown off; behind the butter-dish
Two Gunners kneel, whose gun has disappeared;
A Grenadier with busby and red coat
Mounts guard before a half a pound of cheese.
Some infantry with bayonets fixed begin
A slow advance towards the table edge.
Conscripted from another time and place
A wild Apache waves his tomahawk.
It's all a game. Upstairs, my youngest son
Roars like a little Stuka as he dives
Through dream, banks steep, then cuts his engine out,
Levels, re-enters the armistice of sleep.

War Cemetery, Ranville

A still parade of stone tablets,
White as aspirin under the bland
Wash of an August sky, they stand
In exact battalions, their shoulders square.

I move slowly along the lines
Like a visiting Commander
Noting each rank, name and number
And that a few are without names.

All have been efficiently drilled,
They do not blink or shift beneath

163

My inspection; they do not breathe
Or sway in the hot summer air.

The warmth is sick with too much scent
And thick as ointment. Flowers hurt,
Their sweetness fed by dirt,
Breathing in the dark earth underneath.

Outside the cemetery walls
The children play; their shouts are thrown
High in the air, burst and come down
In shrapnel softer than summer rain.

The Soldier's Dream

After the late shouts, the silences
Shattered like windows, rises
The bugle's husky hymn;
After the boozers' fumbled voices,
Their studs on stone, songs and curses,
The hard blokes are dumb.

After the last fag doused, small brightness
Crushed by the heel of darkness,
Lights out: the night commands.
After groans and expectorations,
Creakings like an old ship's timbers,
Sleep condescends.

In that consoling ambience
Images with unsoldierly elegance
Advance and are recognised.
After the day's gun-metal,
The khaki itch, such softness beckons,
Intentions undisguised.

Such challenge yet complete submission,
Small arms that need no ammunition
Beyond being feminine;
And other naked limbs, much longer,
Cancel parades, the day's loud anger,
With their own disciplines.

And after the cordite's lethal sweetness,
Reek of oil on steel, such fragrance,
A delicate silent tune;
And then the white thighs' open welcome,
The belly and breasts so suave and silken,
The moist dark between.

The bearded grin of generation
Calls the idler to attention,
Rouses the martial man,
Renews him as annihilator,
Restores his role, the man of leather,
Sinew, muscle, gun.

Muzzle flash and blast, bright blaring
Of the bugle of the morning,
The dream and darkness fled;
Orderlies of light discover
The soldier struggling with the lover
On the snarled, dishonoured bed.

Stanley's Dream

The village hall was changed: someone had moved
The church pews into it. There were many people there.
It was a summer evening, fragrant from
Anthologies of flowers. He could not see
All faces clearly, though one he saw quite plain:
Thomas Ashman, the carpenter from Trent.

But Thomas had been dead for eighteen months.
Or had he? Stanley was no longer sure.
Maybe he had dreamt that Thomas died,
For there was no mistaking that grained face,
And no one could deny he was alive
Since he was beckoning with urgent hand.
Stanley waved back and went across the room.
Then Thomas showed that he should bend his head
Close to his secret whisper. Stanley bent,
Then swiftly Thomas grabbed his neck and pulled
His startled face towards his own and pressed
His cheek to his old friend's, and Stanley felt
A coldness like a winter stone. The scent
Of flowers grew intolerably sweet,
The cold bit deep. He struggled to get free
And broke away from that embrace and from
The toils of sleep, but in his waking room
He felt the coldness burning on his cheek
And phantoms of dead flowers explored his throat.

Charnel House, Rothwell Church

I remember the visit now,
See those tiers in the hall of my skull,
The little heads on shelves;
My nose remembers the smell,
Damp and chill, but not rank;
I remember the way they looked down,
Their eyes small, starless caves
In the grey and ochre and brown
Of skulls as cold as stones,
Looked down at the beautiful, neat
Composition of their stacked bones.
What a waste to gaol them away;
I would like some for my friends,
One to give to my wife

Next time I must make amends
For neglect or cruelty.
When I am away from home
It would not be any trouble,
It has no hair to comb.
And if she awoke to face it
Calm on her neighbour pillow
Where tenderly I'd place it
She'd welcome this better fellow,
The lack of fetid breath,
Know any words it could utter
Would have nothing to do with death.

Lives of the Poet

In Spring he saw the hedges splashed with blood;
Rags of flesh depended. In the moonlight
From a chestnut branch he saw suspended
A man who cocked an inattentive ear.
He heard worms salivate and paced his song
To the metronome of the hanging man,
Wore black to celebrate this time of year.

In August, from deceitful beaches, waves
Hauled drowners deeper in; he watched their arms
Wink in the obsolescent sun;
His ears discerned those other melodies
Beneath the chesty self-praise of the band,
The sound of blues. The shifting sand
And sea entombed clean bones, old summer days.

Now Autumn, vicar of all other weathers,
Performs its rites he joins the harvest chorus
At the cider-press and celebrates
In dance of words the seasons' grand alliance,
Puts on his snappiest suit on Friday nights

And stomps gay measures: no dirges now,
For Winter waits with ice and truth and silence.

Legs

Of well-fed babies activate
Digestive juices, yet I'm no cannibal.
It is my metaphysical teeth that wait
Impatiently to prove those goodies edible.
The pink or creamy bonelessness, as soft
As dough or mashed potato, does not show
A hint of how each pair of limbs will grow.
Schoolboys' are badged with scabs and starred with scars,
Their sisters', in white ankle-socks, possess
No calves as yet. They will, and when they do
Another kind of hunger will distress
Quite painfully, but pleasurably too.
Those lovely double stalks of girls give me
So much delight: the brown expensive ones,
Like fine twin creatures of rare pedigree,
Seem independent of their owners, so
Much themselves are they. Even the plain
Or downright ugly, the veined and cruelly blotched
That look like marble badly stained, I've watched
With pity and revulsion, yet something more—
A wonder at the variousness of things
Which share a name: the podgy oatmeal knees
Beneath the kilt, the muscled double weapons above boots,
Eloquence of dancers', suffering of chars',
The wiry goatish, the long and smooth as milk—
The joy when these embrace like arms and cling!
O human legs, whose strangenesses I sing,
You more than please, though pleasure you have
                                    brought me,
And there are often times when you transport me.

Six Reasons for Drinking

I

'It relaxes me,' he said,
Though no one seemed to hear.
He was relaxed: his head
Among fag-ends and spilt beer.
Free from all strain and care
With nonchalance he waved
Both feet in the pungent air.

II

'I drink to forget.'
But he remembers
Everything, the lot:
What hell war was,
Betrayal, lost
Causes best forgot.
The only thing he can't recall
Is how often before we've heard it all.

III

'It gives me the confidence I lack,'
He confided with a grin
Slapping down ten new pennies
For a pint and a double gin.

IV

'It makes me witty fit to burst,'
He said from his sick-bed. 'There's nothing worse
Then seeing a man tongue-tied by thirst.
Hey! Bring me a bed-pun quickly, nurse!'

V

From behind a fierce imperialistic stare
He said, 'The reason's plain. Because it's there!'

VI

'It releases your inhibitions,
Let's you be free and gay!'
The constable told him brusquely
To put it away.

Drunk in Charge

We'd had a damned good party in the mess
The night before, went on a bit too long,
I wasn't feeling quite on form next day.
The Scotch I drank for breakfast didn't help.
I'd half a mind to go and see the quack
Except it wouldn't look too good, I mean
Going sick the morning of the big attack.
I soldiered on. I took a nip or two
While Grieves, my servant, laid my doings out.
An idle beggar, Grieves, but not too bad
As long as you administer the boot
From time to time. Certainly the chap's
Devoted to me, follow me to hell
And back he would. I thought I'd feel all right
After a decent shit, a bath and shave,
A breath of air, but nothing did much good:
Guts still complained, I couldn't see too well.
I took another nip before I mounted.
I rode out well enough and told my men
I knew they wouldn't let me down today—
Stout fellows, every one of them. We trotted off.
We heard the cannon of the enemy
Begin its din. We reached the starting line.
The bugle called. This was the time to show
My quality. I lit a long cheroot,
Pulled out my sabre like a long thin fish
And shouted, 'Charge!' My damned cheroot went out.
'Hold on, my lads! Hold on!' I lit it up
And roared again through its blue fragrance, 'Charge!'

My chestnut stumbled and it nearly fell.
I spurred him on but he reared up and tried
To throw me—a lesser rider would have gone.
I almost lost my long cheroot. I tried
To make him gallop but he wouldn't run.
Either he was lame or else a coward.
My squadron overtook me, thundered past,
Those gallant troopers, surging on towards
The wall of cannonade and musketry,
Hot for a glorious death or victory,
Fine fellows, splendid soldiers every one,
And not a smoke between the lot of 'em.

Not a Bad Life

I am my own hero and I worship me.
Often I loom at night outside the women's conveniences
And mumble through the bullets of my teeth.
When I spit, the leech of phlegm
Spawns a litter of condoms in the gutter.
I am not queer. I shall sleep
In bed soundly, deaf to the day's grum music
Which cannot disturb my repose.
When day slumbers
And the tolerant night gets up
I follow my customary employment:
I am a traveller
In ladies'
Undergrowth.
The commission is generous
And the wages are not derisory,
Could be called, I think,
A pretty good screw.

Polling Day

Politics, said Bismarck, are not
An exact science. Neither is science,
At least it's not to me.
Towards each of these important matters
My attitude is less than reverential
Yet I accept that one cannot deny
The relevance of both, not now
Especially as I approach the booth,
Once more prepare myself
To make this positive, infrequent act
Of self-commitment, wishing that I could
Do more than scrawl a black anonymous mark—
The illiterate's signature
Or graphic kiss—against my favourite's name.
Incongruous, one thinks;
But is it so? In my case not entirely
Since I am voting unscientifically
For one who might be midwife to a dream
Of justice, charity and love
Or scatter obstinately truthful seeds
On these deceitful plots.
No argument or rhetoric could lend
My gesture and my hope more confidence,
So oddly apt this cross, illiterate kiss.

The Winter Man

I

Numb under the fresh fall
The stone of pavements did not feel
The blunted heel. Parked cars were furred
With ermine capes of recent snow;
Substantial silence showed both tint
And texture, bandaging the town

In lint of winter.
                              Looking down
From a window in a high warm room
A man recalled how, once before,
The slow hypnosis of the snow
Had veiled his senses in a trance,
How that pale dance composed its own
Spectral music and deceived—
When the sewing flakes had ceased—
With its white lie, a fraudulent
Paradigm of innocence.
And now, once more, the town wore white,
But he knew well the cold could kill,
That this bland lenitive possessed
No healing skill, would soon be soiled
And, like discarded dressings, show
The old wounds underneath, unhealed.
He did not trust the lying snow.

He turned away, sat by his fire,
A man of thirty-four, unsure
What stance to take, poised as he was
Precariously between the traps
Of youth and middle age; he feared
In equal parts the anguish of
Youthful passion and the absurd
Attitudes of ravenous love
Adopted by the man too old
To play the Prince with word and sword;
And yet he craved such exercise,
Yearned for the natural warmth it lent,
Half believed he could survive—
Without being too severely hurt—
Just one more non-decision bout.
He picked up his book but had not read
A page before the stillness jerked,
Pierced by a double jet of noise
Blurting through the silent room,
Official as a uniform.
The black shell raised, he said no more

Then half his name before a voice
Breathed close; he could have sworn he felt
The warmth of every whispered word.
She knew she did not have to say
Her name, less individual
Than that soft signature of sound.
He said: 'It seems so long ago,'
And thought: How long? A year, or more?
Impossible to measure such
Desolation, so much hurt.
It seemed so long ago . . .

II

Clock and calendar would both agree
That it was fourteen months ago when he,
Bored on a snivelling November night,
Stale as old crust, unable to read or write,
Called on some friends who would not aggravate
His subcutaneous itch, might mitigate
The threat of an enveloping despair.
When he arrived, at once he saw her there,
And all else in that room, human or
Inanimate, whatever dress it wore,
Was darkened and diminished by the claim
Her presence made, a solitary flame
Brilliant among spent ashes of the day.
Although the clock and calendar might say
That moment lifeless lay a year away
He reckoned otherwise: its essence stayed
Fixed in the heart, whatever else betrayed.
And other things remained to tantalize,
Awaken thwarted hungers and surprise
With half recaptured joys: a ride—
So trivial occasion to provide
A charge of such excitement and regret—
A ride in leather dusk when fingers met,
Uncertain for a second, then they clung
Miming longer limbs as if they'd flung
All clothing off; those moving hands amazed

With conscious nakedness and praised
Each other's strangeness and audacity.

Other minute events he could recall,
Gestures of lust and tenderness so small
No onlooker would know they had occurred.
And yet it was not long before he heard
A harsh inflection in her voice and she
Revealed impatience that could rapidly
Become contempt for all he seemed to be,
And had his reason not been on its knees
He would have known, however he might please
Her eyes and mind and flesh on friendly days,
He never could possess her and must face
The truth that her desire was spiked with hate.
So when, as winter laid down arms to spring,
The season when, in fiction, everything
In nature welcomes lusty grooms and brides
But is, in fact, peak time for suicides,
He realised, once the first raw pain had eased,
Like a man informed he's mortally diseased,
Her words confirmed what he had always known:
In spring she turned indifferent as stone
And told him that the time had struck to go,
Her winter love had melted with the snow.

For days he dozed, bemused, and then began
The ache that trailed him like a Private Eye
To cafés, bars, surprising him with sly
Disguises in the street or public park,
Tapping his line, transmitting in the dark
Messages whose sense he could not quite
Seize before each cypher slipped from sight.
He found, again, he could not read or write.
Down avenues of summer, lovers walked;
The green tongues in the trees above them talked
A language that endorsed their bodies' speech,
Yet with the sun's connivance could not reach
Those icy fetters clamped on feeling's source.
And when sun paled with Autumn's sick remorse

And leaves swam in the morning milk of air
As smoke from garden bonfires rose like prayer,
He was unmoved; until fresh winterfall
Prepared white silence to sustain that call
Thrilling the waiting stillness of his room,
A double blade that stabbed with hope and doom.

III

He said, 'It seems so long ago,'
And waited, holding to his ear
The black shell in which low susurrus
Rose and fell, a dream of surf.
He would not go.
Yet even as intention shaped
He felt it melt, a single flake
Of snow that settles on warm stone.
Slowly he lowered the telephone,
Found his coat, switched off the lights
And went down to the white, stunned street.
The coldness glittered in his eyes.
Beneath the stroking wind the fur
Of snow was riffled, then smoothed down.
The stars were frozen chips of flint.
The flesh grew warm, his eyes were bright.
Anticipation drummed and strummed;
Uncertainty sniped at his heart,
Premonitory fear was sharp
And lingered on the tongue, although
A sweeter taste was there also,
Wafer of hope, a desperate joy.
His footprints trailed him through the snow.

THE LOVING GAME
1975

The Loving Game

A quarter of a century ago
I hung the gloves up, knew I'd had enough
Of taking it and trying to dish it out,
Foxing them or slugging toe-to-toe;
Keen youngsters made the going a bit too rough;
The time had come to have my final bout.

I didn't run to fat though, kept in shape,
And seriously took up the loving game,
Grew moony, sighed, and even tried to sing,
Looked pretty snappy in my forty-drape.
I lost more than I won, earned little fame,
Was hurt much worse than in the other ring.

Wicket Maiden

It is a game for gentle men;
Entirely wrong that man's spare rib
Should learn the mysteries of spin.

Women should not be allowed
To study subtleties of flight;
They should bowl underarm and wide.

Or, better still, not bowl at all,
Sit elegant in summer chairs,
Flatter the quiet with pale applause.

It shouldn't happen, yet it did:
She bowled a wicked heartbreak—one,
That's all. God help the next man in.

Enemy Agents

Expert in disguise and killing-blows,
Fluent in all languages required,
They wrote me ardent letters, but in code.
My vanity and ignorance combined
To make me perfect victim for their game.
I took them at face-value every time.

Repeatedly they practised their deceits
And I was fooled, but slowly I became
Alert and learnt few things are what they seem,
Few people, too; so I grew narrow-eyed
And wore suspicion's habit like a coat.
I boasted not just second but third sight.

But then the top man, whom I'd never seen,
The power above the throne as you might say,
Assigned a partner to me. I could see
At once that she was candour's self, her whole
Demeanour spoke of truth. I'll never learn.
Most ruthless of the lot, her cover blown.

Where Shall We Go?

Waiting for her in the usual bar
He finds she's late again.
Impatience frets at him,
But not the fearful, half-sweet pain he knew
So long ago.

That cherished perturbation is replaced
By styptic irritation
And, under that, a cold
Dark current of dejection moves
That this is so.

There was a time when all her failings were
Delights he marvelled at:
It seemed her clumsiness,
Forgetfulness and wild non-sequiturs
Could never grow

Wearisome, nor would he ever tire
Of doting on those small
Blemishes that proved
Her beauty as the blackbird's gloss affirms
The bridal snow.

The clock above the bar records her theft
Of time he cannot spare;
Then suddenly she's here.
He stands to welcome and accuse her with
A grey 'Hello'.

And sees, for one sly instant, in her eyes
His own aggrieved dislike
Wince back at him before
Her smile draws blinds. 'Sorry I'm late' she says.
'Where shall we go?'

Separation

They stand still as trees
In the drifting mist
Of an autumn evening,
Silent as elms
With branches becalmed,
All language drowned,
A man and a woman
Quite motionless,
Yet the space in between
Is slowly increasing.

No gesture from either,
Regret or farewell,
As the interval widens
And they wait for the night
In stillness and silence,
For the moon's blind stare
Or the seal of darkness.

An Anniversary

Endlessly the stream slides past,
Jellies each white flat stone
Which stares through its slithering window at
The sky's smeared monotone.

Two willow leaves glide smoothly on
The water's shimmering skin:
Inches apart they float along,
The distance never changing.

Once, on a branch in the sun, they danced
And often touched each other;
They will not touch each other again,
Not now, not ever.

Marriage Counsel

Your problem is not unusual,
Indeed its absence would be that
(Regard this room as a confessional,
Nothing you tell me will leak out).
So far, it seems, your principal trouble
Is your wife's indifference, her failure to hear

Whenever you speak, in bed or at table,
Her remote and unrecording stare.
These are not uncommon features of a marriage,
In fact the contrary would be true.
You suspect an urgent need for copulation
With an unknown someone, the opposite of you?
She puts black stuff round her eyes and wears
Unaccustomed underclothes,
Ambiguous, weightless as mist? She dyes
The grey bits of her hair and shows
A strange new taste for vulgar romantic songs?
None of this need suggest another man.
You say she has never had strong lungs
Yet, despite Government Health Warnings, she has begun
To smoke cigarettes—expensive, King-size.
It may be the menopause, although
Her new vocabulary might give cause
For perturbation. It could show
That she is being refashioned utterly,
Which certainly suggests a mentor, a new friend.
In this case you must try to be
A different person too. It need not be the end.
Re-woo her. Win her hand again.
And if you fail—which might well occur—
This reflection should ease the ensuing pain:
Consider—you will not really have lost her
Because, from all you say, she is other
Than the woman you married. She is remade.
In this case you have never possessed her
And cannot therefore be betrayed.
Later, the former, the familiar wife
May return. It has often happened before.
But, if she does, do not expect life
To be suddenly charged with honeyed splendour
And harmonious chords. You must not be surprised
If you find your need and passion are dead.
There are times when defeat is to be prized
Above victory.
    Good day to you. You will forget
All I have said.

When Love Has Gone

When love has gone
This at least, or most, stays on:
    When tenderness
Fades and brittles till the press
    Of days destroys,
All arias are pulped to noise,
    Prismatic dome
Drained and stunned, cold monochrome,
    This need remains:
To clamp each other in soft chains,
    The dragging links
Of flesh and, as the last flame sinks,
    In darkness drown
Clinging, bearing each other down.
    And yet, God knows,
You could not tell these cries from those
    That used to flow
When love, it seemed, would never go.

Captain Scuttle Ashore

I've sailed so far and heard the sea's
Drunk shanties rolling under
A moon as fat and powder white
As a spot-lit prima donna.

Black sea ran through my hempen veins;
I drank it down like porter;
My heart was calloused like my hands,
I pissed and bled salt water.

But I'd one pretty whistle in my ditty-box
And, man, the tunes it's played

In knocking-shops and snazzy flats
From Brest to Adelaide.

In shacks and pads and pent-houses
And on the sun-burnt sands,
And once in a Methodist chapel,
I laid them all, like plans.

But this soft inland breeze that sighs
Now I'm ashore for good,
Brings a warm sweet rain that pierces me
As never north sleet could.

And my old concertina heart
Is squeezed by cunning fingers;
No jig or hornpipe rollicks out
But a melody that lingers,

A melancholy air that floats
Through twilight of the blood
And curls around the nervous roots,
Yet is not wholly sad.

There's a kind of joy in the tune that leads
Me to this breathing shore
Where, warm in the briny undergrowth,
I know I'll sail no more.

I'm home at last, I'm harboured now,
Tied up till the day I die,
Held fast by ropes of glossy hair
And anchored to a thigh.

Though white ships round my blue skull glide
And storms bang far and deep,
I'll stay where the waves like lions prowl in
And, tamed, lie down to sleep.

Amities

Amities composed in gentle weather,
Flowering in temperate field or harbouring wood,
Or sealed at ease in warm and fragrant bed

Flinch cravenly when winter swings its axe,
Raise hands in negative surrender when
Threatened by adversity's muscle-man.

It is the friendships built in bitter season,
When menace prowls the street and fields; when food
Is scarce and all you're left to share is need,

These are conjunctions nothing can unmake;
They will survive until all climates merge,
Proof against clock and calendar's furtive rage.

Spot-check at Fifty

I sit on a hard bench in the park;
The spendthrift sun throws down its gold.
The wind is strong but not too cold.
Daffodils shimmy, jerk and peck.

Two dogs like paper bags are blown
Fast and tumbling across the green;
Far off laborious lorries groan.
I am not lonely, though alone.

I feel quite well. A spot-check on
The body-work and chassis finds
There's not much wrong. No one minds
At fifty going the speed one can.

No gouty twinge in toe, all limbs
Obedient to such mild demands
I make. A hunger-pang reminds
I can indulge most gastric whims.

Ears savour sounds. My eyes can still
Relish this sky and that girl's legs;
My hound of love sits up and begs
For titbits time has failed to stale.

Fifty scored and still I'm in.
I raise my cap to dumb applause,
But as I wave I see, appalled,
The new fast bowler's wicked grin.

Self-Inflicted Wounds

Soldiers who decided that
dishonour was a wiser
choice than death, or worse, and spat
into the face of Kaiser
Bill and the Fatherland or
King George's Union Jack
and took up their rifles for
the purpose of getting back
to Blighty by sniping at
their own big toes or trigger-
fingers were called things like 'rat'
but preferred scorn to rigor-
mortis and considered gaol,
for however long, a soft
touch after trench and shell-hole,
but it is only the daft
who think that self-inflicted
injuries hurt less than those
sustained by folk addicted

to being punched on the nose
or greeting mutilation
welcomingly for the sake
of glory and the nation.
The wounds and scars that ache
the worst, and go on aching,
are from blows delivered by
oneself; there's no mistaking
that sly pain, and, if you cry,
you cannot expect a breath
of sympathy; you will find
no healing of any kind
till he comes who began it
all, and cures all, Doctor Death.

The Wrong of Spring

Oh, this risen beauty, treacherous and cold,
Concealing in yellow sleeves its glittering knives
Intended for the tender parts of coves
Who are too old
To dance on green a lithe white measure now,
It is unbearable—well, almost so.

And we grey inconsolables remain
Immured in winter's club; each holds his card
Of membership for which he's overpaid,
And through the window
See daffodils and girls, recalling how
We too walked golden there so long ago.

We dare not venture out; the knives are sharp;
The wind, the flowers, those limbs so delicate,
Yes, even they can pierce the faltering heart;
And we are prudent men
Not warmed by dreams of our lost Aprils, nor
By how we longed to be club-members then.

Our Father

'I was surprised,' my old friend said one night
As we sat there with our drinks and talked
Companionably of things
Linked by threads as thin as our grey hairs,
'I was surprised to find, when I was quite
Grown up—ready to try my wings—
Not that I hated Dad,
But there were many lads who claimed that they loved theirs.

'My father really thought that he was God
And sat upon his own right hand—
So that it couldn't see
What tricks the left was up to: sinister
Was just the word for what that member did.
He seriously claimed to be
Pure beyond reproach:
Pure hell the punishments he would administer.

'A sadist, liar and a fornicator
And, worst of all, strict temperance man,
The perfect hypocrite.
Not once do I recall a single word
Of kindness or affection from dear pater:
He was, in short, a total shit.
I never saw him smile
Far less laugh out; oh yes, he was a walking turd.

'Perhaps you think that I exaggerate,
Oedipal loathing has upset
My power to see the man?
Not so: I saw him on his dying bed.
I feel for him more pity now than hate;
I wish him peace. He lay in sweat
And silence for nine days,
Then spoke. "I'm sorry!" were the last words that he said.'

Wish You Were Here

The sun's brass shout is muffled by a wad
Of woolly cloud; this wind has wandered from
An earlier mood, say March.
Its energy has no good humour in it.
It floats a shiftier beach a foot above
The firm original,
Insinuates grit in sandwiches and eyes.

In spite of drifting sand, a muted sun,
We all, in our own ways, apply ourselves
To this, our annual task
Of relaxation or more active pleasure.
A yellow plastic ball bobs out to sea;
Young men with muscles prance
Or pose and touch their bulges pensively.

They do not touch my heart, as children do
Whose serious play is wholly lacking that
Self-consciousness that robs
The body's speech of plausibility.
The children ply their spades with diligence
Or dare the slavering waves.
Unknowingly they mould a memory.

The old are unselfconscious too. The wives
Lie back in deck-chairs, eyes tight-shut against
The wicked wind-blown sand.
Their husbands, bald and bracered, sleep until
The pubs renew their welcome, opening
Their doors like loving arms.
Incontinent and feline, seagulls yaup.

And I, who feel I'm neither young nor old
But obsolete, lie on my bed of beach
And feel the sabulous wind
Spreading its thin coarse sheeting over me.
Ambition, hope, desire are cold. I'll stay
For sand to cover me,
Forgotten culture, not worth digging for.

A Circle of Animals and Children

The first animals spoke in the darkness,
Comforting. They uttered very simple words.
Their fur was familiar and their names
Easy to say. They had small eyes that never blinked.

I loved them, if love is being grateful
For their presence in my bed. This could be so.
They never disobeyed and seldom hid—
Teddy, Bunny and Jumbo with hide of velvet.

Next came the animals who could not speak:
The hamster, rabbits and cocker-spaniel
That looked like a black compassionate judge
Who would sentence no one. I loved him and liked most dogs.

Until my first child was born. This changed things.
All my delighted tenderness, fear and joy
Were concentrated through a burning-glass
Of gratitude and awe. I had no love to spare.

I watched my son, saw him learning to love,
The first and fumbling rehearsal conducted
Among my old, almost forgotten pets
With chronically astonished eyes. He spoke with them.

And later, predictably, I saw him
Banish the animals who had shared his bed
And take to his heart a brisk terrier,
Giving the little yapper love for a season.

Until his first child was born. This changed things.
He left, with wife and baby, for New Zealand.
Later, my other children went away.
I was alone with time for animals again.

They are company through the winter evenings
By the fireside. They walk with me in summer.
I spoil them, solicit their tolerance,
My mongrel—black dog—and the animal of death.

Our Pale Daughters

When our pale daughters move in lamplight
Their long hair, black or golden, flows
And waterfalls on shoulders, eyes

Contemplate a time and place
That never was nor will be, whose
Trees bear bells and dreams of veils.

But when our daughters move in daylight,
Their locks dammed up in scarves, they see
No trees or white lace in their street

But prams and dustbins, stubbled chins,
And hear cold choristers with lungs
Of steel singing of piston-rings.

Night Music

Darkness and the unceasing sigh and hush
Of the sea, sleepless below the bedroom window,
The slow and gentle molestation of the waves
Fretting the sand and pebbles, soothe the ear
Dismissing grit and sniggers of the day's
Vexations and perplexities, drowning
Those last invaders of the heart's repose.
   And then,
From the room beneath, the punctual music wakes:
Loved and loving hands walk thoughtful on the keys
As mother plays. Now sky and sea are wild
With bells and stars as bright arpeggios rise;
Silver scales—crunched moonlight—move in shoals
Beyond blind nets that reach into the dark.
The child swims through the window into sleep.

The Cowboy of the Western World

He rode into town one summer evening
As the bloodshot clouds presided over
The end of day, the leisurely pacing
Of decent citizens, most of them sober,
Though many intent on altering that.

He left his mount outside the saloon
And swaggered inside and called for liquor;
He felt that every eye in the room
Was fixed on his dangerous challenging figure;
He tilted the insolent brim of his hat.

His pants were tight and his heels were high,
Though his shirt was a temperate but sexy black.
He lit a cigarette, took another slug of rye,
Glanced round the joint then casually
Checked on his weapon with a nonchalant pat.

He stayed for an hour, but met no challenge.
Outside, the sky wore badges and spurs
Enough for a posse; a luminous orange
Spilt light on the sidewalk. When the shooting occurred
He was snug and dreaming in his bachelor flat.

Right Dress

Slither of silk like temperate water over
The humps of hips, delicious as a drink;
Lace froths on flesh as lightly as a shadow
And nylon shines, a sly translucent pink.

Next, the sheer stockings smoothing over knees,
Stretched taut at calves and plumping full of thighs.
The curtains at the bedroom windows press
Back, like constables, the straining eyes.

The sweet and private ritual of dressing,
This beautifying of the self, creates
A painless sense of being loved and loving,
A perfect equilibrium of states.

The frock floats like a fall of mist and roses
Over soft secrets, desiring and desired;
Before the wardrobe mirror gravely poses
Archibald Fullblood, Brigadier, retired.

The Poet's Tongue

With industry and patience he must bring
Together his great arsenal which stores
Blunt cudgels with the very latest thing,
Romantic swords employed in ancient wars
And complicated engines needing great
Skill and practice to manipulate.

And he must travel far in time and space,
Find loot in labs and factories, soil and sand,
Arrange his plunder in well-ordered ways
So what he needs will always be at hand.
And yet, possessing such elaborate means,
He'll constantly invite a puzzled stare
By using—not his intricate machines—
But bits of flint that hit the target square.

One That Got Away

I was alone, desultory line
Drifting in slow-pacing water
When suddenly I felt the tug,
Saw silver twitch in darkness shine

For no longer than a quarter
Of a second. Again, small jerk and drag

And momentary glitter: I knew I could
With skill and vigilance hook this one.
But then I was distracted by
Commotion on the bank where stood
Friendly idlers in the sun
Who, laughing, waved to catch my eye.

Politeness, or a slippier wish
To be esteemed, persuaded me
To greet them, swap some casual chat,
And then they left; but now my leash
Of line was slack; my prey slipped free.
I knew I could not win it back.

I wonder if another man
More serious, luckier than I,
Is richer for my careless loss,
As here in *The Angler's Rest* I stand,
Arms and tongue too short to try
To show how vast and marvellous it was.

NEW POEMS
1975-80

Two Variations on an Old Theme

Winter returns, white with patient rage;
Its peckish minutes nibble at my skin.
I am not old enough to cope with age.

Most men mature, grow stoical and sage,
Don't flinch when, as the knives of ice go in,
Winter returns, white with patient rage.

But somehow I have never reached the stage
Where I can take time's punches on the chin;
I am not old enough to cope with age.

No games divert, no medicines assuage
The pain and fear; my overcoat is thin.
Winter returns, white with patient rage.

Mordacious winds come howling from their cage.
There's no escape, I'm pinioned by their din.
I am not old enough to cope with age.

The little space left on the final page
Attends words like 'deceased' and 'next of kin'.
Winter returns, white with patient rage;
I am not old enough to cope with age.

2

It has to come, I know, but I need time;
I'm not prepared; I've got so much to learn.
I couldn't face it with a face like mine.

The soldier is conditioned by his trade:
He treats the whole thing as a family joke.
The airman tells me it's a piece of cake.

The gaunt religious welcomes it with joy,
Flings wizened arms ecstatically wide
And swallow-dives into the awful void.

Gangsters, cops and nurses every day
Observe its policies without a qualm;
For them the end's the last move in a game.

But wait a minute! What about the kids,
Twelve-year-olds, scared aunties, timorous clerks?
All have faced it; surely they've no tricks

I'm unaware of that could make it seem
Less terrible? No, no, yet most have made
Astonishingly little fuss indeed.

If they can take it, there's no reason why
I shouldn't too. I'll be okay, I know—
Oh Christ, I'll always be too young to die!

Old Man in Winter

The cold time again. The seasons dwindle.
The years contract, and yet each day
Is just as long as past days were,
But not the years. Spring flirts and flaunts,
Impatient for the consummation
Of the Summer. It comes,
Is passionate, then langorous,
Heavy with scent and sleep before
The Fall's inexorable tristesse.
But now the winter moils.
My fire is almost out;
The soft white ash still holds
A little warmth though I perceive
No visible sign of heat,
No sanguine glow. The hour is late.

I hear the brawling wind outside
Shaking the branches of the dying elm,
And I am shaken, too,
But subtly, not as the tree is thrashed
By the gale's insensible rage;
A dudgeon more malevolent
And sly perturbs my brittle boughs,
And I, unlike the elm,
Know that my branches shake, and why.
The room grows cold. Now I must climb
To where sleep, wife-like waits.
Another day dies like the fire.
Succeeding seasons shrink.
The years contract, and yet each day
Is just as long as past days were.
Tomorrow may wear snow. I hope
It will, though no more than a tree
Could I say why I wish this to be so.

Reformed Drunkard

He wakes in a new world and wears new eyes;
His tongue is sweet, as if all night
Summer rain has been his drink
And has rinsed his gaze. His razor moves
With confidence around a temperate smile.
He puts on laundered clothing, knows that vigour
Is stored like legal tender in his purse;
His motion is exemplary, moreover
His wife now wears a different face.
That stare of apprehension and reproach
Has disappeared; she looks on him with pride,
Especially when at dinner he declines
Without perceptible distress or effort
His host's warm invitation to take wine.
She smiles, approving, with the smallest nod;

He is her favourite child. The vicar, too,
Approves, has even stated publicly
That he admires the man, regards
His abstinence as evidence of courage.
The vicar is wrong. Courage or its absence
Is irrelevant.
                          Sometimes, not only in his sleep,
He dreams about that other world, returns
To shiver in a grey chemise of sweat.
What he feels is mainly fear, but something more—
Mixed in that pathogenic stew
Are flavourings of desire, relief, regret.
Something warns him not to analyse
The potency and quantity of each.
He walks a straight line very carefully,
Step by step, day by day. It will lead,
He believes, where all lines lead,
But that is not
For him to think about, far less to say.

A Partial View

It floods the world, it surges like the sea,
Unnecessary suffering that men
Inflict on other men, and equally
Ubiquitous the pleasure felt by them,
Those specialists in pain who busily
Immerse themselves in grave research to find
New strains and modes to benefit their kind.
Steve Biko's agony was someone's joy
Who found delight in witnessing a mind
And body, both superior to his own,
Broken and wasted wantonly. Each slug
That smashes through the knee-cap of a boy
In Ulster is a sweet addictive drug
To him who grasps the gun; the scream or moan

Is transcendental music to the thug.
Neat bureaucrats of systematic death,
To outward view impassive and stone-eyed,
Were tremulous and sticky underneath
Smart tunics when they practised genocide.
When hanging by the neck was used to cure
The anti-social habits of the poor
And solve the problems of the men who kill
From passion, lunacy or greed, forever,
A mob of eager aspirants would fill
The market-place petitioning for the prize,
The office of Chief Executioner.
We live in violent times and always did.
The history of the globe is soaked in blood
And excrement, and we do not improve.
My local paper recently described
An incident in a Wessex seaside town:
A little boy, five years of age, was found
Howling in a public lavatory.
His prick had been cut off, this surgery
Performed by one young man assisted by
Two comrades who held fast their helpless patient.
The operation done, they speedily
Departed on their rasping motorbikes.
This scene poisons the sick imagination:
Their laughter darkening the afternoon
Like burning tyres. Black stench. Say what you like,
There's not a day that breaks that is not strewn
With pain and wreckage, smeared with blood and pus,
Reeling with rage and blind brutality.
Of course I know this is a partial view
That fails to take account of those, like us,
Who represent the great majority,
The decent who deplore such cruelty.
For every act of violence we could find
A score of altruistic deeds performed;
Most people, fundamentally, are kind
And hate to see the humblest creature harmed.
If true it is quite understandable,
This pity for the poor, solicitude

For those who are deprived and are unable
To help themselves; in offering them aid
We re-affirm the human; our reponse
Is rational and we are sane, although
Precariously so. How can we know
That our apparently well-balanced stance
Is set upon foundations firmly laid?
Who knows what levelling stroke is, even now,
Being planned by human evil or the weather?
Indignation may have steamed the glass,
Our vision lost the power of seeing how
Atrocities need not dress up in leather;
Not every yobbo mutters broken type
Nor swings a fist with knuckles made of brass.
The public outrage cannot be concealed;
There is a kind of candour, though not willed,
In blatant executions in broad daylight
That might deflect attention from the plight
Of tortured victims in quiet drawing-rooms,
From libraries where prisoners are grilled
By soft-voiced experts, ruthless and polite,
And from those murders in the afternoons
To chink of teacup and the chime of spoons.
It drowns the children's weeping in the night.
God help us, who are we to act the judge
When fantasies of vengeance warm the blood
And we are gripped by passions we condemn?
We live in violent times and always did.
Tenants of this universal slum
We clamour for a more salubrious home
Yet know that what we are is where we live
And vice-versa. Mankind has not become
Much wiser in its umpteenth million year,
Or gentler, or more generous or just;
More sly perhaps and hypocritical.
Napalm and laser-beam replace the spear,
The ignorant plague gives way to clever dust,
Our language laced by words like 'overkill'.
No nation yet has ever won a war
Yet wars are fought despite the monstrous cost;

Some murders it would seem are ethical.
What is there then to do or say about it?
We could of course anticipate the end
Which mocks all striving yet without which life
Would be unthinkable and all its treasures
Dross, the oldest enemy and friend,
Meet him by way of bullet, gas or knife
Or kinder overdose; but these are measures
Providing answers only to the blind,
Completing the mad circle of destruction.
The rich can build elaborate defences,
Surround themselves with various distractions,
Enlist a corps of connoisseurs and ponces
To cater for their still discerning senses
Or, less sophisticated, they can choose
The blurred and stumbling cul-de-sac of booze
To join at last the swelling exodus
Of imigrants who daily put to sea
Bound for the Happy Isles and lives of bliss,
Utopias of total lunacy.
Our graveyards and insane asylums bear
Plain witness to the popularity
Of stratagems like these. And as for prayer,
The chance of supernatural intercession
Must be at least unlikely, and indeed
Why should God—whose notions of compassion
Have often seemed ironic—intercede?
So what is left? The little consolations
Of human love? Take her to the seaside,
Stand by the window in the sweet night air
And promise to be true to one another.
Yes, why not? But there is something more.
While you stand there swapping vows and kisses,
Hearing the ocean's long withdrawing roar,
Remember that you could be listening to
More varied music than that salty cadence.
When sick and hot from too much of the world
Immerse yourself in pure consoling art,
Press forehead to the coolness of a fugue,
Invite the wordless message to unfold

Its insubstantial scrolls of filigree.
There's always music. But should you wish to hear
The less transcendent language of the tongue
Then choose the harmonies of poetry
Which builds small barricades against confusion;
Or better, be a dancer at their wedding,
Discover there a nostrum for despair,
And unexpected joy that drowns foreboding,
And find yourself, with almost no surprise,
Accepting everything, rejoicing even
That all is as it is, not otherwise;
Though when the music fades and meanings blur,
The hordes remass, you turn again to her
To whom you might conceivably be true
As she, against the odds, might be to you.